MACKINTOSH FURNITURE

From the Library of

MACKINTOSH

FURNITURE

ROGER BILLCLIFFE

LUTTERWORTH PRESS

Produced by Cameron Books,
  2a Roman Way, London N7 8XG
Published by Lutterworth Press,
  7 All Saints' Passage, Cambridge
© Cameron Books, 1984

Reproduction by Tenreck Limited,
  172a Brent Crescent, London NW10
Printed by BAS Printers,
  Over Wallop, Stockbridge, Hants
Bound by R.J. Acford,
  Chichester, Sussex

Printed in England

ISBN 0-7188-2564-0 (cased)
ISBN 0-7188-2565-9 (paperback)

Edited by Ian Cameron and Jill Hollis
Designed by Tom Carter

The sources of archive photographs are given in the captions, except for pictures reproduced from magazines of the period. The photograph of the completed bedroom for the Dresdener Werkstätten is from a brochure for the magazine *Deutsche Kunst und Dekoration* kindly loaned by Albert Albano of the Philadelphia Museum of Art.

Most of the other photographs were specially taken for *Charles Rennie Mackintosh: the Complete Furniture, Furniture Drawings and Interior Designs* by Eric Thorburn, Graham Metcalfe and Ian Cameron, or provided by Glasgow University or Glasgow Art Gallery & Museum. Pictures of the reconstruction of the Southpark Avenue house, including those used on the jacket or cover, were taken for this book by Douglas Corrance. Other new photographs appear by courtesy of The Fine Art Society, Christie's and Sotheby's.

Much of the material contained in this book is based on Roger Billcliffe's full *catalogue raisonné, Charles Rennie Mackintosh: the Complete Furniture, Furniture Drawings and Interior Designs* (Lutterworth Press), and the numbers in the picture captions are those of the catalogue entries in that work. Each entry number includes the date of the object or interior plus a reference number for a piece of furniture or a reference letter for an interior. In the latter case, the collection mentioned in the caption is that for the photograph and not for the items of furniture.

CONTENTS

INTRODUCTION 7

EARLY FURNITURE & INTERIORS, 1892-97 11

TEA ROOM & DOMESTIC DESIGN, 1896-98 23

THE WHITE ROOMS, 1898-1900 37

THE VIENNA SECESSION &
    THE HAUS EINES KUNSTFREUNDES, 1900-01 67

WINDYHILL & KINGSBOROUGH GARDENS,
    1901-02 79

THE TURIN EXHIBITION
    & THE WÄRNDORFER MUSIC SALON, 1902 89

THE WILLOW TEA ROOMS, 1903 101

THE HILL HOUSE, 1903-04 115

HOUS'HILL, 1904 135

SOUTHPARK AVENUE
    & COMMISSIONS, 1904-06 149

GLASGOW SCHOOL OF ART WEST WING
    & TEA ROOM DESIGN, 1907-11 165

WORK FOR W.J. BASSETT-LOWKE
    & OTHERS, 1916-20 191

BIBLIOGRAPHY 219

INDEX 221

INTRODUCTION

In the fifteen years before the outbreak of war in 1914, Charles Rennie Mackintosh was better known in Europe than in Scotland, or even in Britain as a whole. Among British architects, only M.H. Baillie Scott equalled Mackintosh in the extent to which his designs were publicised and imitated in Europe. However, Mackintosh's reputation did not rest on his achievement as an architect, since his most important building, the Glasgow School of Art, never received coverage under its designer's name in any publication either at home or abroad and was known only to the small group of his friends who had visited Glasgow and returned home to tell about it. Even his two major houses, Windyhill and The Hill House, both of which were covered in journals abroad, were admired at least as much for their interiors and furniture as for their external features and planning. It is apparent from Mackintosh's commissions abroad that it was as a designer of furniture fully integrated with its setting that he was so well received. Exhibition rooms, interiors and individual pieces of furniture were sought after by his European clients and colleagues, but he never designed anything abroad on the scale of Windyhill, let alone that of the Glasgow School of Art or Scotland Street School.

Mackintosh himself would not necessarily have considered his interiors and furniture designs less important than the design of complete buildings. His approach was the same whatever the size of the commission; there are as many surviving drawings for a single spoon as there are for a complex chair, as many for the interior of a bedroom as for the exterior of a whole house, and all are executed with the same care, using no less skilfully applied washes, so that they are as much works of art as the objects they represent. In Mackintosh's view, architecture was the consummate art, encompassing all others; he did not consider himself merely a designer – he was an architect and, as such, responsible in his buildings for all the arts, many of which he did in fact practise, in particular being an accomplished watercolourist. Mackintosh's interiors and furniture were crucial elements in his buildings; the interiors were, after all, the areas in which his clients spent most of their time, and he went to great lengths to ensure that the planning of the rooms fuctioned well and that the design pleased the client before he began serious work on the exterior elevations.

The idea of working from the inside out became a Modern Movement cliché, but for Mackintosh it was an article of faith. This did not necessarily mean that the external massing was totally dictated by internal arrangements, for Mackintosh was not so short-sighted a designer that he would fail to consider the project as a whole. Indeed, dated drawings indicate that the final decorative schemes and detailed designs for furniture were devised when the structure was almost completed, as at The Hill House, where the interior settings all date, at the earliest, from the autumn of 1903, when the house was almost finished. However, the interiors were obviously not afterthoughts, no matter when the detailed final designs were produced.

While the exteriors indicate the internal division of the house and the functions of its separate parts, the decorations and furniture enhance the rooms, emphasising each particular function and delighting the eye.

Mackintosh designed well over four hundred pieces of furniture in a working life of only twenty-five years. This number seems all the more impressive when one considers that the great majority of the designs are contained in the periods 1897-1905 and 1916-18, and that there is very little repetition of any one design (unlike, for instance, the stock designs that C.F.A. Voysey repeated over and over again). The vast majority of the designs were domestic in scale, and most of the commissions included very detailed interiors – in the seven years from 1900, interiors and their furniture account for the bulk of Mackintosh's output with the exception of the Willow Tea Rooms, Scotland Street School, Windyhill and The Hill House. Virtually all the interiors were designed with the same total control over the varying elements in the composition: chairs, tables, hat-stands, beds, wardrobes, clocks, mirrors, carpets, wall decorations, light fittings, keys, even cutlery and cruet sets – all came out of the same fertile imagination that was also controlling structural steelwork and sophisticated ventilation systems and could deal with the planning of a large art school and the design of a three-roomed gatehouse, not to mention churches and even gravestones.

Unlike Josef Hoffmann, who had access to the Wiener Werkstätte, or C.R. Ashbee, who had the Guild and School of Handicraft, both employing gifted artists and craftsmen, Mackintosh produced his interiors and furniture using local tradesmen, furniture makers and joiners like Francis Smith or Alexander Martin, who were running ordinary businesses rather than idealistic craft workshops. Although his craftsmen had been trained to the highest standards of workmanship in the Clyde shipyards, his designs had to be understood by men who were not accustomed to making art furniture. That they failed to convince Mackintosh of their superior knowledge of furniture construction is shown in the poor condition of many of the pieces today. What made Mackintosh different from an Ashbee or even a Hoffmann was his concern not with materials, craftsmanship or construction but only with final appearance. Perhaps no guild-like body of artist-craftsmen would have worked with him, and he might not readily have tolerated the pursuit of traditional methods and materials for their own sakes. In fact, the only artistic manufacturer or collaborator he consistently used was his wife, Margaret Macdonald, although her influence and assistance had an appreciable impact only during the years 1901-03.

Mackintosh was not an Arts & Crafts designer, as the Arts & Crafts Exhibition Society made all too clear when his work was accepted for their 1896 exhibition. It was not the last time Mackintosh exhibited with them, for he showed at their next exhibition, in 1899, and again in 1916, but it was probably a crucial experience for him as a young designer, and he must have decided that the ways of the Arts & Crafts movement were not for him after seeing the 1896 show.

His earliest designs do show some evidence of enthusiasm for the guiding principles that made the Arts & Crafts movement so attractive to the younger generation of architects and designers. J.D. Kornwolf has admirably summarised the movement's aims: 'First, and most obvious, the Arts and Crafts emphasised the artistic potential of everyday objects. Second, vastly higher standards of craftsmanship were applied to these objects, and the ideal of craftsmanship was realised much more widely than had been possible before. . . Third, new stress was given to the importance of function in the creation of forms – what Voysey was to call "fitness for purpose".' Mackintosh readily accepted the first and the third of these principles, but 'craftsmanship' was for him too often synonymous with old-fashioned methods of construction. If traditional craftsmanship stood between him and the realisation of a design, then it was craftsmanship that had to go. This has meant that many of his pieces have not stood the test of time and that, in Glasgow at least, his furniture acquired a reputation for shoddy construction as well as for inflicting an inhuman lack of comfort. His early furniture is well made, however, at least in the sense that it is sturdy and that it takes cognisance of its basic material, wood. It was not, on the other hand, made with the elegant craftsmanship of a piece by Ernest Gimson or Ashbee or L.F. Day; its structure is often brutally displayed, as it is more the work of a joiner using strong but coarse-looking joints than of a cabinet-maker, who would produce strength and beauty in more equal proportions.

Mackintosh travelled back beyond the Arts & Crafts style of the day to search for the traditional furniture that formed the basis of his work in the 1890s, as it had provided a starting point, too, for William Morris. However, much of the furniture that Mackintosh designed from 1900 to 1918 does not have an easily identifiable source, and it becomes increasingly difficult to relate, say, the contents of the Wärndorfer Music Salon to the vernacular tradition. While Voysey remained within that tradition or expanded on it, Mackintosh moved away from it.

In his biography, Thomas Howarth has pointed out the influence of Japan on Mackintosh. In his basement room in 1896, Mackintosh hung up reproductions of Japanese prints. The houses depicted in them would undoubtedly have had a great effect upon him, particularly in the inter-penetration of spaces and the use of open screens and partitions. The careful positioning of furniture within a space and its delicate relationship with the vases of twigs and flowers that decorated his rooms are perhaps the most important elements of Japanese style to be seen in his work. The unerring skill of the Japanese in assembling a perfectly balanced composition from straight lines and simple forms interacted with Mackintosh's own imagination to produce a totally new style.

The white furniture of 1901-03, however, was not at all Japanese in inspiration. Its symbolism derived from European literature and painting – from the Pre-Raphaelite Brotherhood, Aubrey Beardsley, Jan Toorop and Maurice Maeterlinck. The visual and literary images of these artists' works were synthesised by Mackintosh, who added to them his own particular genius. The result was a style with recognisable roots, the individual motifs of which can be traced to specific sources, although the final effect is nonetheless individual and inventive. It is the work of a man aware of the past but not wishing his work to be dominated by it; it was Mackintosh's solution to the *fin-de-siècle* problem that faced so many artists, writers and architects – the search for a new style, independent of the past, through which to express modern ideas.

The age of the 'free style', as it has come to be called, had no greater exponent than Mackintosh. Glasgow, Barcelona, Vienna, Brussels, Darmstadt, Paris and Chicago all produced their own free-style designers, many of whom sought the same solution as Mackintosh and almost achieved it. Only in Chicago was there a genius as receptive and, at the same time, as inventive as Mackintosh. Frank Lloyd Wright and Mackintosh never met, but their furniture design shows strange parallels up to about 1901. If there was any interchange of ideas through journals, it can only have been in one direction, because Wright's work was not published in Europe until 1910, while Mackintosh's work would have been known in America through the magazine *The Studio*, which was readily available there.

Chimneypiece in the Smoking Room, The Glasgow Art Club. 1893.B.

EARLY FURNITURE & INTERIORS, 1892-97

From 1889, Mackintosh worked in the architectural practice of Honeyman & Keppie in Glasgow. His early work there on interiors can first be glimpsed in two of the firm's commissions for remodelling existing buildings. In both cases, John Keppie was the partner in charge of the job, and he was undoubtedly responsible for the choice of style, but the details were left to Mackintosh. In the first of the two jobs, the remodelling and extension of the Glasgow Art Club's premises, for which the designs were commissioned in 1892, the rather debased classical style was Keppie's, but the rich ornament was the work of Mackintosh. The somewhat perverse treatment of classical features, notably the strange columns of the fireplaces (repeated in the second commission, Craigie Hall), did not reappear in Keppie's work after Mackintosh began to concentrate on commissions of his own. Yet while the only drawings that survive for the project are in Mackintosh's hand, it cannot be classed as truly one of his designs, but is rather to be

The Glasgow Art Club. *Left:* The Smoking Room. 1893.B. *Right:* Chimneypiece in the Smoking Room. 1893.D.

seen as his personal response to the limitations of an established office style.

Craigie Hall was designed by John Honeyman in 1872 for Thomas Mason, a Glasgow master builder who was responsible for building many of the large villas in the Pollokshields and Dumbreck areas. The commission for alterations to the entrance hall and library in 1893 was dealt with by Keppie, but again the decorative detail leaves no doubt that Mackintosh was responsible for the design of the fittings. The most obviously avant-garde features are the four doorcases in the hall, with their stylised pilaster architraves and the overhead panels of carved foliage and flowers. In the library, the restrained pattern of leaded glass again suggests Mackintosh's hand rather than the more florid style of Keppie. The pediments and capitals have a stylised tongue motif, which is also seen on the *Glasgow Herald* building in Mitchell Street – another Keppie and Mackintosh joint project. Much of the carved decoration, with its distortion of natural forms such as flowers and stems and even birds' wings, must have been detailed by Mackintosh, and the face on the side of the fitted armchair is so close to some of the Spook School watercolours that it leaves no doubt as to the authorship.

There is hardly any precise documentary evidence to support dating of the furniture designed between 1893 and 1897. As little of Mackintosh's work was exhibited or illustrated before 1896, it is possible to be definite only about dates before which the pieces must have been made. Thomas Howarth has recorded the memories of Mackintosh's friend Herbert MacNair about how he started to design furniture, and there is little doubt that Mackintosh would have followed MacNair's example (even if he had not initiated the technique himself). By placing tracing paper over illustrations of furniture in catalogues or magazines, MacNair would try to improve on the original design or devise new forms of decoration for it.

Left: Bookcases and fireplace in the library, Craigie Hall, Glasgow (mahogany, French-polished, with panels of leaded glass). The carving on the end of the bench and the pattern in the leaded glass are typical of Mackintosh's Spook School work of the period. *In situ.* 1893.4. *Right:* Detail of bench end. 1893.4.

For David Gauld, Glasgow painter and stained-glass designer. *Top left:* Washstand (oak, stained green). A very simple piece, enlivened only by the use of simple curves. Designed as a wedding present for David Gauld. 1893.5. *Top right:* Wardrobe (oak, stained green), the largest of the pieces for Gauld. An otherwise conventional design, this wardrobe is the first item to use stylised, almost abstract, carved decoration in the shape of a bird's head – a frequently used motif over the next few years. 1893.6.

Bottom left: Dressing table (oak, stained green). 1893.7. *Bottom right:* Ladderback chair (oak, with rush seat). Although associated with both the Gauld furniture and other pieces for William Davidson, it is still possible that this is a commercial piece and not designed by Mackintosh at all. 1893.8. All Hunterian Art Gallery, University of Glasgow.

This practice probably accounts for the somewhat traditional shapes of what is probably the earliest known furniture designed by Mackintosh, the bedroom suite that he gave as a wedding present to David Gauld in 1893. By reducing commercial designs to their basic outlines, he would have arrived at the plain, simple massing of elements in these pieces. He still used bead mouldings to define different parts of the composition, but machine-made ornamentation has been entirely eliminated, and the designs depend for their effect on broad expanses of wood relieved by a little carved decoration and simple metal fittings. The timber is oak and its broad grain is emphasised by the dark green, glossy stain applied to it. The designs for David Gauld are not particularly successful, but, as an attempt to avoid the overloading of moulded and machine-run decoration that characterised most of the furniture then being made commercially, they are an impressive beginning.

The remaining early furniture falls into three groups: for William David-son's house, Gladsmuir, at Kilmacolm; for the firm of Guthrie & Wells; and for his own or family use or for his buildings, principally the *Glasgow Herald* offices. The Gladsmuir furniture was probably produced over a period of about three years, from 1894 to 1897. Stylistically, the earliest piece is an alcove cabinet that fitted into a recess next to the drawing-room fireplace. Like the other furniture from around 1894, it is in the same vein as the pieces for David Gauld, with simple beaded mouldings but otherwise only hand-carved decoration and panels of glass featuring organic motifs in the leading. Mackintosh was not yet able to rid his designs of all traditional forms of decoration: on the Gladsmuir cabinet and on a bookcase that was possibly made for Mackintosh himself in 1894, a strangely detached *cyma recta* capital is used. In the cabinet, there is also a completely new motif that can only be described as four apple pips around a central post in an inset form in the shape of a giant apple. Organically inspired decoration was characteristic of Mackintosh's furniture for the next ten years. Roses, trees, birds, cabbages, apple pips, tulips, bulbs and corms were all noted in his sketch books and provided a vocabulary that was used for much more than the furniture: watercolours, posters, fabrics, beaten metal panels and, above all, architectural sculptures were based on the natural shapes that he drew in the countryside, the garden or the kitchen. Organic decoration gradually replaced the traditional mouldings and beads, although the *cyma recta* capital remained a favourite device for some years to come.

In about 1895, Mackintosh was commissioned by Guthrie & Wells, a Glasgow firm of decorators, cabinetmakers and stained glass manufac-turers, to design bedroom furniture for them. This went a little further along the lines that he had been following at Gladsmuir, but, probably because the furniture was intended for commercial production, there were no major changes in style. The emphasis remained on broad, unmodelled expanses of timber, relieved only by metal handles and hinges. It is not known how popular the designs were, but certainly no examples have come to light apart from those owned by William Davidson.

In a number of other items, Mackintosh began to develop a more individual style. The simple stained timbers and metal fittings remained, but there

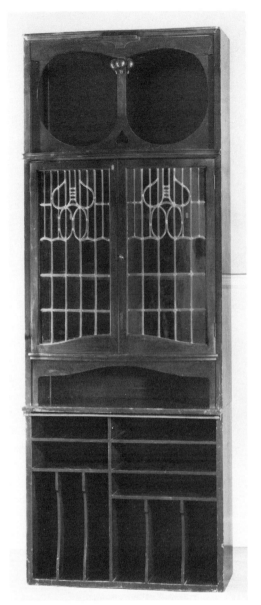

Left: Cupboard for Gladsmuir, Kilmacolm (cypress, with glazed doors). The organic motifs in the leaded glass are echoed in the representation of a giant apple in the pierced shape over the doors, which has a cluster of apple pips (or stylised birds' heads) around the central post. The Fine Art Society. 1894.1. *Above:* Bookcase (cypress, French-polished, with glazed doors). The use of a detached *cyma* *recta* capital and the pattern in the glass doors recall the cupboard (1894.1). 1894.2. *Below:* Wardrobe (cypress, stained dark, with brass hinges and handles). A very simple design, probably made by Guthrie & Wells, Glasgow. 1894.3.

were also *repoussé* metal panels and more varied outlines and decorative details than had been evident in the Guthrie & Wells pieces. One such design is the large settle that was probably made specifically for the 1896 Arts & Crafts Exhibition, where it was offered for sale. The stylised plants stencilled on the back-rest, and the lead panel showing three peacocks

Above: The Museum, Queen Margaret Medical College, Glasgow. The use of an upper gallery over the main Museum floor looks forward to the first plan for the Library for the Glasgow School of Art drawn in 1896. 1895.B.

would have contradicted the effect of the rest of the settle, with its sturdily utilitarian appearance. The panel, in particular, was all too easily identifiable with the metalwork exhibited at the same time by the Macdonald sisters which was anathema to the Arts & Crafts Exhibition Society, being, they thought, too close to the depravity of Art Nouveau.

The outcry against the Glasgow exhibits must have affected the impressionable Mackintosh, but I doubt that it was the cause of the widening difference in appearance between his furniture and the products of the Arts

Opposite page. Left: Dressing table with mirror (cypress, stained green, with brass handles). Bought by William Davidson for Gladsmuir, this piece appears in the Guthrie & Wells catalogue for c.1896. Glasgow School of Art. 1895.2. *Top right:* Wardrobe. Commissioned by Guthrie & Wells, this piece is a simple development of 1893.6 but it might have been painted white. Untraced. 1895.1. *Bottom right:* Washstand (cypress, stained green, with brass handles and tiled top). This design shows a gradual move away from the more conventional work of earlier years. Glasgow School of Art. 1895.3. *This page. Left:* Hall settle (oak, stained dark, with beaten lead panel and stencilled linen upholstery). Exhibited at the Arts and Crafts Exhibition Society in 1896, this settle incorporates the largest of the decorative metal panels that Mackintosh was to use in his furniture. National Museum of Antiquities of Scotland. Edinburgh. 1895.5. *Top right:* Linen press (oak, stained green, with brass handles and candlesticks and two beaten lead panels). All the traditional details of the cabinetmaker,

such as bead mouldings, have been stripped from this design, which is perhaps the most successful of the early works. Glasgow School of Art 1895.6. *Bottom right:* Jewel box for Jessie Keppie (wood, mounted externally with beaten sheet brass and set with pieces of opalescent glass). Mackintosh broke off his close friendship with Jessie Keppie c.1896 and transferred his affections to Margaret Macdonald, whom he later married. Victoria & Albert Museum, London. 1895.8.

& Crafts movement. Both the settle and the linen cabinet for John Henderson, which was also made in 1895, indicate that he had already begun to experiment with more expressive and symbolic motifs. For a year or more, these continued to take the form of applied patterns or *repoussé* panels, but gradually the expressive line and sculptural massing spread out from individual details to the whole piece. Few pieces displayed the imagery of the Spook School (as the Glasgow designs were christened by the Arts & Crafts movement), but the symbolism inherent in such decoration came to encompass the entire design.

In an article in *The Studio* in 1895, M.H. Baillie Scott wrote: 'It is difficult for the architect to draw a fixed line between the architecture of the house and the furniture. The conception of an interior must naturally include the furniture which is to be used in it and this naturally leads to the conclusion that the architect should design the chairs and tables as well as the house itself. Every architect who loves his work must have had his enthusiasm damped by a prophetic vision of the hideous furniture with which his client may fill his rooms, and which looks all the more incongruous if the rooms themselves are architecturally beautiful.' If Mackintosh had enjoyed the same access to the press as Baillie Scott, he would doubtless have published similar statements, but, in January 1895, he had had the opportunity neither to write about such interiors nor to design them.

Mackintosh's room in the family house at Regent Park Square, Glasgow, shows how he wished to control fittings like fireplaces and to design the

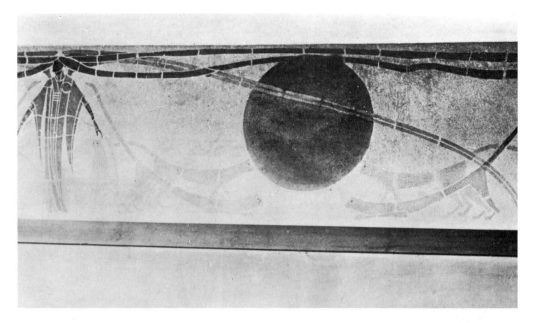

Opposite page: Contemporary photograph of Mackintosh's bedroom at 27 Regent Park Square, Glasgow. This photograph shows several features – such as the use of wallstraps, dark papered walls, stencilled friezes – which were to be regularly used in later interiors.
1896.A. *Above:* The nursery at Gladsmuir, Kilmacolm. Mackintosh has repeated the stencil decoration used in his own bedroom.
1896.B. *Left:* Bed (cypress, stained green). Designed for Mackintosh's own bedroom at 27 Regent Park Square, Glasgow School of Art.

1896.2. *Right:* Sideboard/drawing cabinet (oak/stained dark, with brass handles and hinges). Probably the first piece of furniture designed for his own use. The combination of a *cyma recta* moulding topping square columns was to be used many times in the future. Hunterian Art Gallery, University of Glasgow. 1896.1.

decoration as well as the furniture. At Queen Margaret Medical College, Glasgow, he was given his first chance to integrate interior fittings and furnishings with the architecture. Nevertheless, this is still not a fair example on which to base firm conclusions, as the brief and the available funds would undoubtedly have restricted him, as, once again, would the partner in charge of the job, John Keppie. The structure was completed in 1895, and the interiors would almost certainly have been designed in that year. Although the furniture is simple and unexceptional, the pierced motifs on the ends of the benches indicate Mackintosh's involvement in the design. The panelling on the walls and the overall dark tonality of the interiors also suggest his hand. Indeed, the interiors have a distinct similarity to those designed for the Glasgow School of Art at the end of the following year, when cost was again a major factor. The interiors at the School of Art, however, were

Left: Chest of drawers (cypress, stained green, with brass hinges), made by Guthrie & Wells, probably to match the bed. Glasgow School of Art. 1896.5. *Right:* Table (oak, with brass handles) for the offices of the *Glasgow Herald*, Mitchell Street, Glasgow. The downward projection on the stretchers and the aprons of the table betray the involvement of Mackintosh in a piece obviously influenced by the taste of John Keppie, who supervised the *Herald* job. Glasgow Art Galleries and Museums. 1896.6. *Below:* The Editor's Room at the *Glasgow Herald*. 1896.B(i).

probably reworked in 1899, because they are far more refined than the rather traditional fittings at the Medical School.

Much of the furniture so far described is relatively simple and not fundamentally different from that of the Arts & Crafts movement. Parallel with these pieces, though, were produced the series of more adventurous, almost experimental designs, which have in common the incorporation of beaten metal panels, either abstract or figurative in pattern, and an attempt to get away from the rectangularity of Mackintosh's other furniture. The first of these is probably an 1895 design for a bookcase, which still has a number of quite conventional features, but is heavily overlaid with stylised plant forms, presumably intended for execution in metal relief rather than in carved wood. It is difficult to date the others with any certainty, although a tentative order might be: first, the linen cabinet for John Henderson, where the long stems with heart-shaped leaves are reminiscent of the jewel box for Jessie Keppie (whom Mackintosh deserted for Margaret Macdonald in 1896) and the raked apron with its central pendant leaf motif anticipates the more subtle curve of the 1896 sideboard; second, the hall settle made by Guthrie & Wells in 1895; third, the linen press for William Davidson; finally, the writing desk for Gladsmuir, made in 1897.

Left: Linen press (cypress, stained green, inlaid with coloured woods and white metal, and metal handles), designed for William Davidson. The metal strapwork is the most elaborate of any piece of the period, reflecting the freedom which a client like Davidson gave to Mackintosh. Glasgow School of Art. 1896.8. *Right:* Cabinet for the offices of the *Glasgow Herald* (oak, with brass handles and locking plate). This design combines practicality with typical Mackintosh motifs like the pierced gables of the cabinet and the miniature posts supporting the top. Glasgow Art Galleries and Museums. 1896.7.

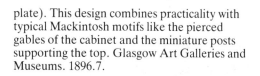

Gladsmuir, Kilmacolm. *Above left:* Schoolroom table (pine, stained dark). The thistle motif in its gables is repeated in the bookcase. 1897.3. *Above right:* Bookcase (cypress, stained dark, with two beaten brass panels and glazed doors). The two metal panels first appeared on the design for a fender (1896) and were later re-used at Westdel in 1898. 1897.2. *Centre left:* Desk with hinged top (oak, stained dark, with beaten metal panel and brass handles). A simple design, similar to much of the Argyle Street furniture but distinguished by a *repoussé* panel on the lid. 1897.1. *Centre right:* Side table (oak, stained dark). Stylistically this table dates from the period 1897-99, but it was first illustrated in 1902 in an article on Windyhill. 1897/9.6 *Below:* Schoolroom bench (pine, stained dark). 1897.4. All Glasgow School of Art except 1897/9.6 which is untraced.

TEA ROOM & DOMESTIC DESIGN 1896-98

It was not until William Davidson asked him to prepare plans for a new house at Kilmacolm around 1899 that Mackintosh received a domestic commission combining architectural and furniture design. This was Windyhill, for which the furniture was designed in 1901. In the preceding years, however, Mackintosh had designed a few pieces for Queen's Cross Church in 1899 and had undertaken several schemes for the conversion and decoration of interiors, including the design of the furniture. The largest and most important of these commissions was the Argyle Street Tea Rooms, where he designed furniture for the owner, Catherine Cranston, in 1897.

Mackintosh's first work for Miss Cranston in 1896 was for her Tea Rooms at 91-93 Buchanan Street, a street of fashionable shops which was one of the city's main thoroughfares. She had acquired the premises in 1895 and had commissioned George Washington Brown of Edinburgh to rebuild

Buchanan Street Tea Rooms, Glasgow. *Left:* A dining-room. T.& R. Annan, Glasgow. 1896.I. *Right:* Stencil decoration in the Ladies' Tea Room. These are the most elaborate stencils that Mackintosh was ever to make, combining elements of Spook School design within a more architectural framework. T.& R. Annan, Glasgow. 1896.C.

Stencil decoration in the Luncheon Room, Buchanan Street Tea Rooms, Glasgow. T.& R. Annan Glasgow. 1896.E.

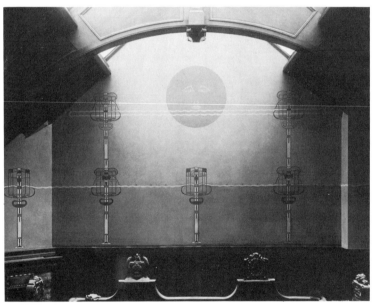

Stencil decoration in the Smoking Gallery, Buchanan Street Tea Rooms, Glasgow. T.& R. Annan, Glasgow. 1896.F.

A dining room at the Buchanan Street Tea Rooms, Glasgow. The stencils in this room are by George Walton, but the light fittings correspond to a drawing in one of Mackintosh's sketch books. T.& R. Annan, Glasgow. 1896.G.

them in 1896; they were opened to the public in the summer of 1897. The results were not outstanding, and Gleeson White, writing in *The Studio* in that year, declined to mention the architect's name because the building had suffered much criticism. Miss Cranston commissioned the designer George Walton to oversee the decorations and the provision of the furniture for Buchanan Street, and all this work was carried out by his own firm. It is not known whether it was Walton or Miss Cranston who asked Mackintosh to produce designs for stencil decoration of the walls in the Ladies' Tea Room, the Luncheon Room and the Smokers' Gallery. The Tea and Luncheon Room extended around an open well containing a staircase, and Gleeson White described how its background colours of green, 'greyish-greenish yellow' and blue could be seen as a progression from earth to sky.

The decoration of the Ladies' Tea Room was inspired by a Mackintosh drawing, *Part Seen, Imagined Part*, dated April 1896 and now in the collection of Glasgow Art Galleries and Museums. This drawing was translated into a frieze of tall figures arranged, not in repetitive rows, but in pairs facing each other across a stylised tree. These statuesque ladies are dressed in white, their heads silhouetted against a gold nimbus and their bodies wreathed in tendrils of stylised plants. The trees reappear in the Luncheon Room, this time arranged in groups of five between broad pilasters painted with representations of peacocks. The totem-like trees here all look alike and have tops that are variations on the theme of formalised leaves and flowers. In the Smoking Room on the top floor, the trees have been reduced to the most basic and skeletal forms, even more totem-like than those in the Luncheon Room and connected mysteriously by a rippling line, which is repeated in a double form at a higher level, where it runs across a circular sun or moon with drooping eyes, a nose and lips. All this work was carried out by Guthrie & Wells; the colour was applied in flat, graduated washes, but the uneven plaster surface caused the paint to shimmer with light.

It was probably by choice rather than from lack of opportunity that Mackintosh's decorative work was rarely on this scale again, except in his tall banners at Turin in 1902. The Buchanan Street decorations relate closely to the poster designs that Mackintosh produced in the mid-1890s, using similar imagery and the same large-scale elements, and posters were an art form that Mackintosh did not return to after 1900.

The Buchanan Street commission gave Mackintosh his first major opportunity in interior decoration. Mackintosh had used small stencils for his own bedroom and in the Gladsmuir nursery, but here they were intended to stand out from their surroundings (just as his posters were), to clamour for attention amid the distractions of other designers' work. In this, they undoubtedly succeeded, for it is Mackintosh's decorations that are remembered rather than Walton's sensitive but not particularly original furniture or the heavy details of Brown's architecture. In most later commissions, Mackintosh had control of all the elements of the design, and he was not faced again with having to compete with the work of others except at the Turin Exhibition, where he was to use figures almost twice as large as those

Smoking Room, Argyle Street Tea Rooms, Glasgow. Mackintosh designed the movable furniture and George Walton was responsible for the panelling, screens and stencil decorations. 1897.A.

Luncheon Room, Argyle Street Tea Rooms, Glasgow. Mackintosh designed the movable furniture and George Walton was responsible for the panelling, screens and stencil decorations. 1897.B.

Billiards Room, Argyle Street Tea Rooms, Glasgow. Walton designed the billiards tables, the fireplaces and the stencilling and Mackintosh the other furniture and the lights over the billiards tables. 1897.C.

Billiards Room,
Argyle Street Tea
Rooms, Glasgow.
1897.D.

Luncheon Room,
Argyle Street Tea
Rooms, Glasgow.
Screens and stencilling
by Walton, furniture
and possibly the lights
by Mackintosh.
1897.E.

at Buchanan Street to define and draw attention to the area of the Scottish exhibits.

The roles adopted by Mackintosh and Walton at Buchanan Street in 1896 were reversed a year later at Miss Cranston's other tea rooms in Argyle Street. By this time, the two men were clearly moving away from each other. The rather delicate refinement of Walton was not emulated by Mackintosh, and the furniture for the Argyle Street Tea Rooms demonstrates his more aggressive manner.

All the pieces are made of oak, with an emphasis on broad, unmoulded planes; the timber is sometimes simply varnished or even scrubbed but more often is dark-stained. The tub chairs and the sturdy coffee and dom-ino tables, which are all very heavy and difficult to move, give the impression of having been made of timber straight off the saw. Nevertheless, they do have quite subtle details such as tapering or splayed legs, carved organic decoration, and gently curved strips of timber along structural members to draw a distinction between the carcase of the piece and the less functional in-fill panels. Although traditional details have been entirely eliminated, the constructional methods are normal, which is possible partly because the designs are generous with timber and provide wide enough sections and rails to sustain strong joints.

All the items designed for Argyle Street can be readily identified from their bold outlines and boxy shapes. One chair, however, stands out from all the other designs: the dining chair with a high back and oval back-rail from the Luncheon Room. Where vestiges of Arts & Crafts Movement influence can still be found in most of the furniture at Argyle Street, this design broke away completely from precedent. The function of these tall chairs was to reinforce Mackintosh's conception of spatial composition, defining and dividing the room, which was in an old building converted by George Walton. Although the exaggerated proportions of the chairs can be attributed in part to their function, Mackintosh was obviously interested in the design for its own sake, and he developed the theme of the high-backed chair far beyond functional needs until it became one of the most assured elements in his *oeuvre*. The Argyle Street high-backed chair also introduced the use of laths and a form of natural decoration that is so stylised as to be almost abstract. Springy laths, which give a light and airy impression, were used in several later designs for tea room furniture, while organically based decoration appeared on almost every piece of furniture that Mackintosh designed until about 1904. The decoration of the Argyle Street furniture is by simple cut-outs, often in the shape of a flying bird (as in the high-backed

Below: Domino table. Known only from an illustration in *The Studio*, this clover-leaf table was probably designed for the Argyle Street Tea Rooms. Untraced. 1897.7.

Opposite page. Right: Armchair with ladderback for the Argyle Street Tea Rooms, Glasgow (oak, stained dark). A solid-looking chair designed for the exclusively masculine preserve of the Billiards Room. Mackintosh has simplified what is basically a traditional ladderback chair to produce a powerfully modern design. 1897.9.

Top left: Armchair with low back for the Argyle Street Tea Rooms, Glasgow (oak, stained dark), used in the Smoking and Billiards Rooms. The example illustrated has the rear posts terminated by small knobs, a feature found only on a unique chair which Mackintosh made for his own use. Hunterian Art Gallery, University of Glasgow. 1897.11.

Top right: Circular card table for the Argyle Street Tea Rooms, Glasgow (oak). A variant of a square card table (1897.13, *see* 1900.8, page 52). Glasgow Art Galleries and Museums; Glasgow School of Art. 1897.14.

Right: High-backed chair with pierced oval backrail for the Argyle Street Tea Rooms, Glasgow (oak, stained dark, with rush or horsehair seat). The first high-back chair designed by Mackintosh and one of the most subtle and striking in its shape and the manipulation of traditional woodworking techniques. Mackintosh was so pleased with it that he used a variant of it in his designs for the *Haus eines Kunstfreundes* competition and also in his own dining rooms. Glasgow School of Art; Hunterian Art Gallery, University of Glasgow; Victoria & Albert Museum, London; Museum of Modern Art, New York. 1897.23.

Argyle Street Tea Rooms, Glasgow. *Top left:* Stool (oak, stained dark), used in the Smoking Room. 1897.15. *Centre left:* Upholstered settee (oak, stained dark, upholstered in horsehair). A very sturdy and heavy piece of furniture which was used in the Smoking and Billiards Rooms. Glasgow School of Art. 1897.16. *Bottom left:* Table for the Argyle Street Tea Rooms, Glasgow (oak, stained dark). The device of setting the legs on the diagonal was often used by Mackintosh in later years, but the pierced decoration and the solid construction firmly link this table with the other furniture at Argyle Street. 1897.20. *Right:* Armchair with high upholstered back for the Argyle Street Tea Rooms, Glasgow (oak, stained dark, with horsehair upholstery). An elegant design intended for use in the Ladies' Reading Room. Glasgow School of Art. 1897.19. *Opposite page. Left:* Hat, coat and umbrella stand (oak, stained dark, with metal hooks and drip trays). Another design which Mackintosh was to use in his own houses. Hunterian Art Gallery, University of Glasgow. 1897.28.

chair), or by the addition of raised carved panels – the first time that Mackintosh had used carving successfully.

The Argyle Street work, like that at Buchanan Street, does not appear in the books of Honeyman & Keppie. As several of the drawings are nevertheless inscribed with the firm's address, Mackintosh was obviously able to undertake such private jobs with the knowledge of his employers – perhaps

Argyle Street Tea Rooms. *Top right:* Domino table with quadrant shelves (oak, stained dark). One of the simplest and most practical of Mackintosh's designs, it combines strength of construction with typical details, such as the way the tenons from the legs make a pattern on the table top and an astute use of organic forms, here a clover leaf forming the shape of the lower shelves. Glasgow Art Galleries and Museums; Glasgow School of Art. 1897.22. *Bottom right:* Armchair with pierced side panels (oak, stained dark). One of the most successful of the Argyle Street designs. The pierced shape in the side panel – a stylised flying bird – was also used in the high-backed chair (1897.23). Glasgow School of Art; Hunterian Art Gallery, University of Glasgow. 1897.27.

Above: Side table for the Argyle Street Tea Rooms, Glasgow (oak, with metal handles and decoration). A simple and traditional Scottish design enriched with typical Mackintosh detail in the metal panels. 1897.31.

Left: Chair with curved top rail for the Argyle Street Tea Rooms, Glasgow (oak, stained dark, with horsehair upholstery). A simple chair combining a lower back rail with elements of the high-backed chair. 1897.26. *Opposite page:* Dining room with fitted cupboards and side table for H. Brückmann, Munich. The first recorded foreign commission for Mackintosh. The extensive use of leaded glass, inlaid metal panels and wall stencilling set the pattern for other interiors over the next two years. 1898.A. Cupboards and side table. 1898.1.

his winning the competition for the new building for the Glasgow School of Art increased his status in the office. The Argyle Street furniture was the first large commission in which Mackintosh was unlikely to be restrained either by the tastes of his office superiors or by the rather limited means of such patrons as the young William Davidson. His style flowered at Argyle Street and changed little over the next three years, until the furnishing of his own flat at 120 Mains Street in 1900, a period during which Mackintosh received more domestic commissions, both for whole rooms and for single pieces of furniture.

Rectangular shapes dominated many of his designs up to 1900, with an emphasis on broad panels of timber relieved by gentle curved aprons, pierced or carved decoration and *repoussé* metal panels. These panels were rarely as bold in their relief as those on the hall settle of 1895 or the Gladsmuir desk of 1897, and their imagery turned slowly towards that of Mackintosh's watercolours of the period: delicate and attenuated female figures, often fairy-like and certainly more benign than the malevolent women who appear in the work of the Macdonald sisters. Mackintosh's courtship of Margaret Macdonald was not reflected in his designs at this point: there was little softening of his bold and aggressive forms and (apart from the Brückmann cabinet of 1898) no obvious co-operation with Margaret before the smoker's cabinet of 1899. Even in this piece, her contribution was restricted to the decorative panels and had no real effect on the overall appearance.

Although he produced few new chairs between the Argyle Street commission and 1900, Mackintosh did develop several designs for cabinets and similar pieces. The heaviness of the sideboard/cabinet made for his own bedroom in 1896 was gradually reduced in a series of designs during 1897 and 1898, most of which have one feature in common: they all have overhanging cornices, usually of *cyma recta* profile, often projecting as much as 10 cm. over the front and sides of the body of the cabinet. The doors are sometimes glazed, usually with a pattern in leaded glass, or have *repoussé* metal panels or even an embroidered (or stencilled) curtain. Cabinets like these were used in two small but quite important commissions for the decoration of whole rooms, a dining room in Munich and a bedroom in Glasgow, both dating from 1898.

The dining room for H. Brückmann, editor of the magazine *Dekorative Kunst*, was Mackintosh's first documented commission outside Scotland and one that was almost certainly prompted by Gleeson White's article in *The Studio* in 1897. Some pieces by Mackintosh were illustrated in the November 1898 issue of *Dekorative Kunst*, and it seems likely that the commission for the dining room came during negotiations for the article, probably in the late spring or early summer of 1898. This means that it predates the other major commission of that year, the bedroom at Westdel, as is also indicated by the stylistic evidence, and it initiated a formula for the decoration of dining rooms that Mackintosh followed for several years.

Contemporary photographs show a dark room with fitted furniture and dark-coloured wallpaper reaching up to the picture rail, a white ceiling and a frieze that is also white and has stencilled decoration. Mackintosh was not asked to design the tables and chairs for the room – these were by Karl

Bertsch, but this minor disappointment would have been tempered by the publicity that the commission received. Mackintosh was responsible for the fitted cupboards and side table, the free-standing cabinet and the double doors to the room. The design of these pieces looks back to the furniture for Guthrie & Wells and the Argyle Street Tea Rooms: there is little that is radically different. The decorated frieze, however, was to be used again at Westdel in a different and more successful form, and the large cabinet is clearly a prototype of the smoker's cabinet of 1899. The one completely new departure is the involvement of Margaret Macdonald in the scheme – the two beaten metal panels on the cabinet are probably hers, and the large panel over the side table is definitely one of her designs (an identical one was shown at the Vienna Secession Exhibition in 1900 and another, or possibly the same one, is in the collection of Glasgow University).

Below: Organ case (mahogany, French-polished) for the Music Room, Craigie Hall, Glasgow. The only organ, of the several that Mackintosh was to design, that was actually made. The metal strapwork on the doors and the superb carving on the central column are the best examples of their kind on furniture dating from the 1890s. 1897.45.

Opposite page. Bottom left: Cabinet for H. Brückmann, Munich (oak, stained dark, with beaten metal panels). An important early cabinet. The way that the top of the piece projects widely at the sides and connects with the flanking back panels was to be repeated on many other items in later years. The two decorative metal panels may have been made by Margaret Macdonald and, if so, are the first instance of her direct collaboration with Mackintosh. 1894.4. *Bottom right:* Detail from organ case. 1897.45.

Above: Dining room for H. Brückmann, Munich. 1898.B.

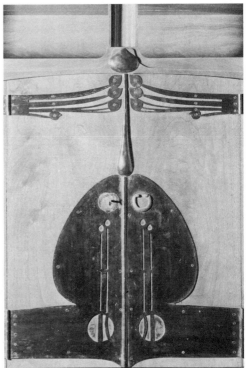

Top left: Detail from organ case for Music Room, Craigie Hall, Glasgow. 1897.45.
Top right: Detail from Organ case. 1897.45.
Bottom left: Fireplace in the Music Room, Craigie Hall, Glasgow (mahogany, French-polished). Although in the same room as the organ (1897.45), this fireplace is designed in the office style of John Keppie. 1897.44.
Bottom right: Organ stool for the Music Room, Craigie Hall, Glasgow (mahogany, French-polished). 1897.46.

THE WHITE ROOMS, 1898-19..

Mackintosh's work had been illustrated in *Dekorative Kunst* in 1898 at the instigation of Brückmann, who was obviously an influential client, and there is no doubt that Mackintosh's reputation would have spread as easily by word of mouth through Brückmann's contacts in Germany and Austria as it would through the rather inadequate illustrations in the magazine itself (the text referring to the dining room was separated by several pages from the illustrations). It was unfortunate, then, that the other commission of 1898, at Westdel, 2 Queen's Place, Glasgow, for another publisher, J. Maclehose, was not illustrated until 1902, again in Brückmann's *Dekorative Kunst*. This bedroom was much more important than the Munich dining room in the development of Mackintosh's mature style. Had it, too, appeared in print in 1899, Mackintosh's reputation as one of the leading furniture designers in Europe would have been established before he participated in the Vienna Secession exhibition in the autumn of 1900.

At Westdel, Mackintosh designed only a second-floor bedroom with a dormer window, and its adjoining bathroom. The room was dismantled and transferred to the Glasgow University collection in 1976, although the bed and the wall decorations had long since disappeared. It was probably designed late in 1898, concurrently with, or just before, the Director's room at the Glasgow School of Art, and a drawing for the scheme was exhibited in Glasgow in January 1899. The frieze was very similar to that used in Munich, but there the rest of the room was rather dark, like most of Mackintosh's dining rooms. The Westdel bedroom, on the other hand, is the first recorded instance of a 'white room' designed by Mackintosh.

This may not have been the first time that Mackintosh actually had his furniture painted – one or more of the Guthrie & Wells designs may have been enamelled white – but it was certainly the first occasion on which all the contents of a room were painted white rather than being simply stained and waxed. The departure was not entirely novel: much so-called art furniture for bedrooms was painted white, and Baillie Scott and Walton had both advocated the choice of white if an architect wished to paint his furniture. Walton had even recommended it as a colour for bedrooms in a lecture in Scotland (probably Glasgow) which Mackintosh would almost certainly have heard. At Westdel, the lower parts of the bedroom wall seem to have been painted light grey or some other pale colour, a treatment that was repeated in the drawing room for 120 Mains Street in 1899-1900. On the whole, the furniture is solid and boxy like the Argyle Street designs, but a

Westdel, Queen's Place, Glasgow. *Left:*
Bedroom. The formula of stencilled friezes
above dark walls is familiar from earlier work,
but this is the first time that Mackintosh has
used white paint in such a deliberate way to
cover all his woodwork. The bed (wood,
painted white) has typical organically inspired
carved decoration, and is a prototype of the
white beds for 120 Mains Street, Windyhill
and The Hill House. 1898.C. Bed, untraced,
1898.15. *Right:* Wardrobe (cypress, painted
white, with two beaten metal panels and metal
handles). A piece that is still very much in the
style of the furniture designed for the Argyle
Street Tea Rooms, but here painted white. The
repoussé panels are identical to others used on
the Gladsmuir bookcase. Hunterian Art
Gallery, University of Glasgow. 1898.11.

Below: Detail from wardrobe. 1898.11.

Westdel, Queen's Place, Glasgow. *Left:* Fine beaten metal panel based on a peacock motif from the fireplace (pine, painted white) echoing the carved motif of the wardrobe. Hunterian Art Gallery, University of Glasgow. 1898.13. *Right:* Dressing table for Westdel, Queen's Place, Glasgow (oak, painted white with metal handles). A more elegant design than the earlier bedroom furniture designed for Guthrie & Wells in 1894-99. Hunterian Art Gallery, University of Glasgow. 1898.17.

number of features point to new interests leading away from the somewhat heavier tea room style.

The carving on the foot of the bed is much more delicate than the bold shapes used in Argyle Street. It takes its form from the wild flowers that Mackintosh sketched at every opportunity as a way of building up a vocabulary of organic details for use in his three-dimensional designs. The gentle curve of the top of the foot-board and the subtle swell of its outer posts both mark a change towards a more fluid style, which is echoed in the ogee curves of the fireside cupboard. The decoration and shape of this cupboard suggests that Mackintosh wanted to break away from the usual associations of wood, and its design is not influenced by traditional wood-working techniques.

In contrast, the wardrobe for Westdel is solidly rectilinear, but again one element of its design points to Mackintosh's apparent desire to force timber to perform unusual, even unnatural tasks. On the upper part of each door, a panel of beaten metal relieves the stark simplicity of the piece; these panels are not fitted flush, but are raised proud of the plane of the doors as if they were framed and sitting on the surface. Even so, they still appear part of the same structure. Mackintosh achieved this effect by raising the wood of the doors around each panel; if the doors had been unpainted, it would have been possible to detect the change of grain and the mitred joints of the raised frames, but, as all the timber is covered with the same hard, white surface, one has the impression that the raised panels simply flow out of the material of the door. In stained timber, the treatment would have had much less impact – indeed, it would probably have been seen as an aesthetic failure. It is acceptable here because the distortion of the wood is not visible. This was one of several such experiments in detailing tried by Mackintosh in his search for a style where the observer would not be aware of the material beneath the paint. A major problem that now faced him was how to come to terms with wood, a material with ancient associations, which was normally used in traditional forms that were dictated by its structural strengths and weaknesses.

Mackintosh's next use of white was not in a bedroom but in the Headmaster's (now Director's) Room at the Glasgow School of Art. The first phase of the School of Art was opened in December 1899, and there is no evidence that Mackintosh departed from his usual practice of designing the movable furniture and fittings in the last few months before completion. Although Mackintosh was working to a tight brief and budget, the interiors and the few pieces of furniture are more advanced than those of the Argyle Street Tea Rooms and are closer to the work at Westdel and at Queen's Cross Church, for which much of the furniture was probably designed in 1899 at the same time as the fitting-out of the School of Art (the building had been designed by Mackintosh in 1897 and 1898 and opened for worship on 10th September 1899).

The Church and the School of Art have the first panelled interiors to appear in Mackintosh's work. At the School, the panelling is simpler, even crude, but the basic unit of broad boards butt-jointed, with a narrow cover slip, is common to both buildings. The wood for both was stained dark, apart from some panelling at the school which was always painted white (the staining has since been removed at the church). The Church panelling, particularly in the chancel, is decorated with carved floral motifs, and the

Left: Roof timbers at 233 St. Vincent Street, Glasgow. A miniature version of the wooden roof structure at Queen's Cross Church and the Glasgow School of Art. 1899.C. *Right:* Panelling at 233 St. Vincent Street. 1899.B.

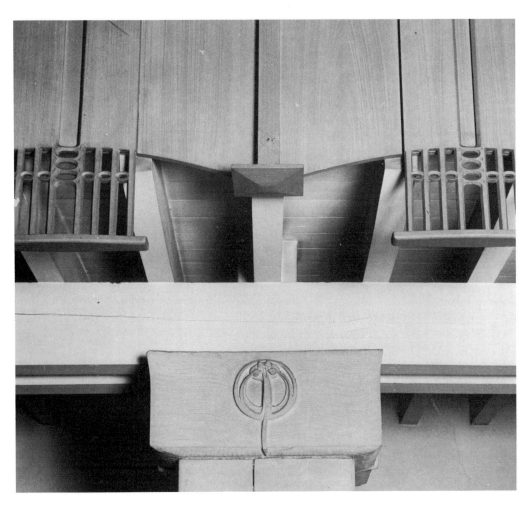

Above: Detail of the pendants in the gallery balustrade, Queen's Cross Church, Glasgow. These pendants look forward to the elaborate carved pendants used in a similar fashion on the Gallery of the School of Art Library in 1909.

1899.D. *Below:* Roof trusses in the hall, Queen's Cross Church, Glasgow. A stylised tree symbolises the strength of the Church and the natural material of the roof itself. 1899.F.

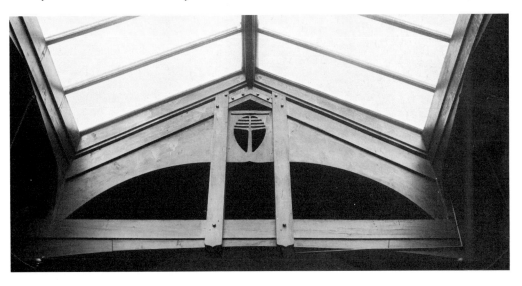

41

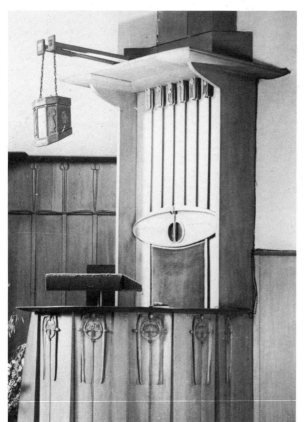

Queen's Cross Church, Glasgow. *Above:* Communion table (oak, stained dark) Mackintosh's version of a medieval, and probably English, altar. 1899.9. *Opposite page. Top left:* Pulpit (oak). The carving of the swooping bird protecting the delicate leaves of the tree brings together many of the images in the church. 1899.8. *Bottom left:* Armchair (oak, stained dark, with horsehair upholstery). 1899.6. *Top right:* Detail of pulpit. 1899.8. *Centre right:* Stand for the collection dish (pine, stained black). The carvings on the sides of this stand show motifs based on birds (also used on the pulpit) and bees. 1899.7. *Bottom right:* Armchair (oak, stained dark, with horsehair upholstery). A very simple design which may also have been intended for use in the Glasgow School of Art. 1899.4.

reredos has stylised tulips on its projecting capitals. Some of the church doors have three tall, narrow panes of glass, above which is often a kidney-shaped panel of coloured glass. A similar motif has been used along the fronts of the two galleries, where it becomes far more elaborate, projecting down below the gallery as an openwork carved pendant, a motif that Mackintosh later used on a number of occasions, culminating in the *tour de force* of the Library pendants at the School of Art in 1909.

Most of the interior of the School of Art is panelled as at Queen's Cross with a *cyma recta* cornice and a low skirting. The main staircase has four square, tapering posts, joined by open balustrading with a single, continuous horizontal cornice, which ignores the rake of the stair. Virtually the only decoration was in the panels of leaded glass in many of the doors and in some pierced shapes in the beams of the Museum roof. In the Board Room and the Headmaster's Room, however, Mackintosh was allowed a little more licence. The original Board Room was in the east wing and was probably never used for its intended purpose, because space was at such a premium in the half-finished building that it was pressed into service as a studio. It contains four tall bow windows and a large stone fireplace. Presumably the surviving pieces of early furniture, an armchair and a settle, were intended for use in this room. However, until the new Board Room was completed in 1906, the Governors met in the Secretary's office.

The Headmaster's Room, the second white room that Mackintosh designed, is altogether more original and ambitious than the Westdel bedroom, which was admittedly somewhat cramped. No movable furniture seems to have been designed for it at the outset, and the Headmaster, Fra Newbery, had to wait until 1904 for furniture to match his surroundings.

Glasgow School of Art. *Left:* Entrance Hall. 1899.G. *Right:* East corridor, photographed in 1910. 1899.L. *Below:* The Museum. Photographed in 1910. 1899.I. *Opposite page. Above:* The Director's Room. This photograph, taken in 1910, shows the armchair which Mackintosh designed for the room; but the rest of the Director's furniture had been taken to the new Board Room. 1899.H. *Below:* The Board Room. This photograph, dating from 1910, shows the original Board Room in use as a design studio. 1899.J.

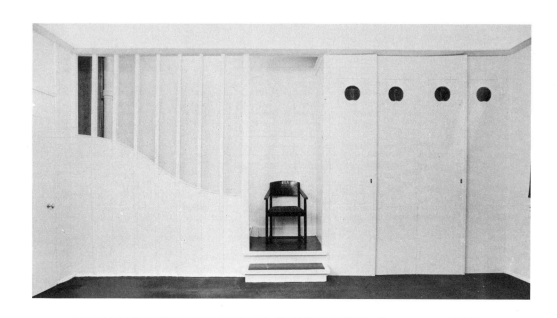

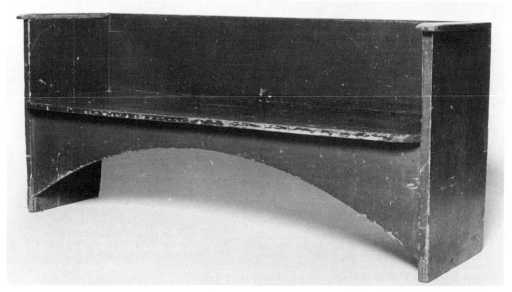

46

Glasgow School of Art. *Left:* Fireplace for the Director's Room (pine, painted white). Mackintosh's version of a traditional design using wrought iron and plain cement renders. The basic design was to be repeated many times but here Mackintosh has provided the room's occupant with a considerable amount of storage space above the grate rather than the decorative panel which he usually incorporated. 1899.11. *Right:* Armchair for the Board Room (oak, stained dark, with upholstered seat). Designed for the original Board Room in the East Wing of the School of Art. Glasgow School of Art. 1899.13. *Below:* High-backed armchair with oval backrail (oak, stained dark, with horsehair upholstery; some with a painted panel set into backrail). A variant of the Argyle Street high-back chair. Arms have been added and some chairs of this design had a decorative panel by Margaret Macdonald inserted in the oval top rail. Copenhagen Museum of Decorative Arts; Glasgow School of Art. 1899.16. *Opposite page. Top:* Fitted cupboards in the Director's Room (pine, painted white, with leaded glass panels and metal handles). The cupboards are fitted into the depth of the staircase, which rises to the private studio above, and maintain the line of the staircase screen balusters. 1899.10. *Centre:* Settle for the entrance hall, Glasgow School of Art (pine, stained dark). Three of these benches were designed to fit the three bays of the Hall. 1899.12. *Bottom:* Settle for the Board Room (oak, stained dark, with upholstered seat). The design is a compilation of three examples of the Board Room armchair without intermediate arms and with the pierced hand-hole motif repeated three times in each back rest. 1899.14. All Glasgow School of Art. *Overleaf:* Detail of high-backed armchair. 1899.16.

Some of the woodwork in the Hall of the School and the interiors of the studios were painted white, but elsewhere in the building the woodwork was predominantly dark. The white paint of the Headmaster's Room, combined with the more generous provision of cupboards and the imposing fireplace, served to indicate the status of the occupant. The shiny white paint, which made the surfaces glint and reflect the good amount of light that entered through the large north window, made the room seem larger and more imposing than it was and at the same time prevented the cupboards becoming too dominant a feature. At Westdel and in the Brückmann room, Mackintosh had had to operate within existing structures, but here he had a greater area to work with and was able to control it completely.

Although the Headmaster's Room is basically a square with a wide bay added along the north side, Mackintosh was able to give it a degree of spatial complexity. The bay has a vaulted ceiling much lower than the rest of the room, and the wall panelling dips in an ogee curve to emphasise its lower height. This end of the room was intended as a business area, with provision for Newbery's desk and even for a dumb-waiter to carry papers from the School Office below. The centre of the room was to be occupied by a circular table (which was eventually provided in 1904). To the east of the desk bay is a cloakroom, the door of which is set into the remaining part of the north wall of the square. On the east side is a staircase to the Headmaster's studio above. This staircase runs parallel with the east wall but behind the line of it, and the integrity of the wall is retained by the use of a panelled screen. The lower half of this is formed in Mackintosh's usual manner of wide boards with cover slips, but a gentle ogee curve cuts across the boards, indicating the rise of the staircase behind. Above the curve, the cover slips become square posts and the spaces behind them are left open to give a view of the staircase and wall behind. The use of vaulted ceilings and open screens to indicate changes of function within an otherwise homogeneous space became a favourite device used with increasing skill and subtlety in later commissions.

Pulpit and choir stalls, Gourock Parish Church, Strathclyde. The design of the carved tracery on the pulpit and stalls is a forerunner of the decoration used at Holy Trinity, Bridge of Allan, in 1904. *In situ*. 1899.18.

Shortly after designing the interiors for the Glasgow School of Art, Mackintosh turned to furnishing and decorating a flat for himself in anticipation of his marriage to Margaret Macdonald in August 1900. This was at 120 Mains Street (now 120 Blythswood Street), Glasgow, and it gave Mackintosh little, if any, scope for structural alteration. However, he was able to experiment with and put into practice many of the theories he had been developing while working on earlier and smaller projects, and the rooms set the pattern for many later decorative schemes. For instance, movable furniture was also painted white, not just in the bedroom, but also in the drawing room, which included his first white-painted chair. The lighting was more atmospheric than any he had used before, with emphasis on candles in the dining room. In the bedroom, he was able to design furniture far more graceful than that at Westdel, but again it was unified and enhanced by the all-enveloping hard white enamel, which was here relieved by inlays of purple, rose and green glass and stencilled hangings of the same colours.

Contemporary photographs show only four rooms – the dining room, drawing room, studio and main bedroom – but the other rooms in the flat probably followed the same general principles. The drawing room was the most important room in the flat, and, given its fixed physical dimensions, the treatment of the walls and windows and the placing of the furniture were masterly. As Thomas Howarth remarks in his biography, 'by contemporary standards the drawing room . . . was positively bare.' The furniture was entirely of the architect's own design, and it was arranged with exceptional care. Mackintosh removed the central rose that had adorned the ceiling, but retained the original moulded cornice. The lighting was provided

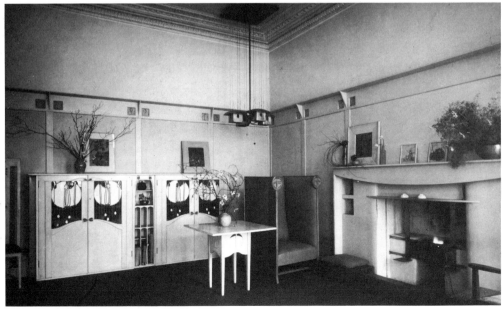

50

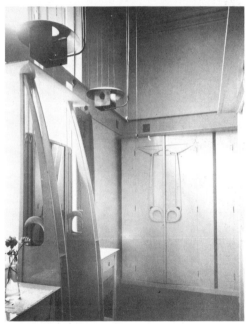

120 Mains Street, Glasgow. *Above:* Studio. Mackintosh seems to have retained the original dado rail but has introduced a shelf at the height of the top of the fireplace. T.& R. Annan, Glasgow. 1900.D. *Left:* Dining room, which follows the now regular pattern for his dining rooms of the dark walls below a pale frieze and ceiling. T.& R. Annan, Glasgow. 1900.E.

Right: Bedroom. A radical development of the white bedroom at Westdel. T.& R. Annan, Glasgow. 1900.F. *Opposite page. Above:* Drawing room. Mackintosh's transformation of a typical Glasgow tenement flat. The careful positioning of the few pieces of furniture, the plain carpet and the white woodwork created a minor masterpiece. T.& R. Annan, Glasgow. 1900.B. *Below:* Drawing room. T.& R. Annan, Glasgow. 1900.C.

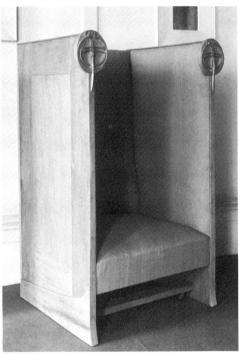

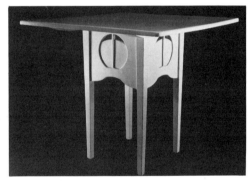

surrounds Mackintosh's version of the traditional cottage grate. Like most of the fittings made for 120 Mains Street, Glasgow, it was transferred to his new house at 78 Southpark Avenue, Glasgow, in 1906. 1900.1. *Left:* Lug chair (oak, with linen upholstery). An extremely simple box-like design relieved only by the applied curve at the base and the two carved plaques. Based on the traditional 'Orkney' chair, this piece was designed to protect its user from the draughts in these large Victorian rooms. 1900.5. *Right:* Square card table (oak, painted white). A white-painted version of the table first made for the Argyle Street Tea Rooms, Glasgow. All Hunterian Art Gallery, University of Glasgow. 1900.8.

120 Mains Street, Glasgow. *Above:* Fireplace for the drawing room (pine, painted white). A large but simple structure composed of broad planes contrasted with subtle curves. It

by three groups of four gas fittings, and a fourth lighting point near the door seems to have been left unused. The skirting, window architraves and door were all retained, but enamelled white, and a broad white rail supporting a flat shelf encircled the room at picture-rail height, even cutting across the openings for the three windows. Vertical straps about the width of the shelf were fixed at intervals between this rail and the skirting, and the large panels thus created between these uprights were covered with light grey painted canvas. The frieze and the ceiling were white. Artificial light was provided by twelve gas jets, each with a square shade, hung in three groups of four.

The furniture was carefully spaced around the room, each piece being allowed, even encouraged, to make its own impact without having to compete with the others. Each of the four walls had some major focal point: a wide fireplace, a double bookcase and a large desk, all painted white, were placed against three of the walls, while on the fourth a dark-stained oval back-rail chair was silhouetted against the grey canvas and framed by the soft light pouring in through the fine muslin that covered the windows. Margaret's embroidered curtains were hung from the picture rail. In the centre of the room, no more than three or four pieces occupied the whole floor area of six metres square. The chairs and tables appeared isolated, but each had its correct, calculated place, so that any change of position would upset the balance of the room.

The dining room was also sparsely furnished, but much darker, and its walls, like those at Munich in 1898, were covered with coarse grey-brown wrapping paper. As in the drawing room, a broad rail, this time painted black, encircled the room at architrave height. On a side wall, against the dining table, two tapering square posts reached up to this rail, carrying

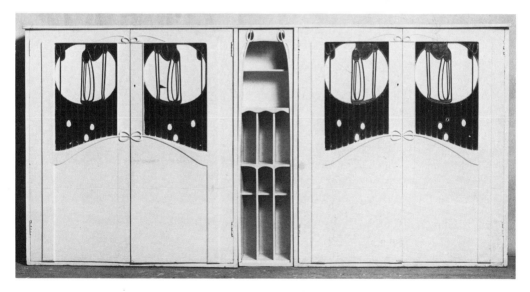

Bookcase for 120 Mains Street, Glasgow (oak, painted white, with leaded glass doors). The most elaborate piece designed by Mackintosh designed for the Mains Street drawing room.

The leaded glass is a *tour-de-force*, the most elegant design in glass that he was to produce. Hunterian Art Gallery, University of Glasgow. 1900.7.

writing desks which usually incorporated some decorative piece of beaten metal, leaded glass or even gesso panels. Hunterian Art Gallery, University of Glasgow. 1900.9 *Top right:* Detail from desk. 1900.9 *Centre:* Dining table (oak, stained dark). A similar table to those used at the Argyle Street Tea Rooms, Glasgow, but embellished with two motifs of double petals on each side. Glasgow School of Art. 1900.20. *Left:* Serving table. Hunterian Art Gallery, University of Glasgow. 1900.21.

Opposite page. Left: Cheval mirror (oak, painted white, with metal handles and inserts of coloured glass). A spectacular piece, compared by a commentator on the Vienna Secession exhibition to a giant sledge placed on its end. Hunterian Art Gallery, University of Glasgow. 1900.26.

120 Mains Street, Glasgow. *Top left:* Desk (oak, painted white, with beaten brass panels by Margaret Macdonald). The first of a series of

candelabra. Above the rail, the frieze and ceiling were painted white. The furniture was simple in design and made of stained oak. The fireplace was painted black, a tall, narrow fitting, more like the bedroom fireplace than the wide, elegant design for the drawing room.

The bedroom and the studio were painted white, as was all of the bedroom furniture. The bedroom, although smaller than the drawing room,

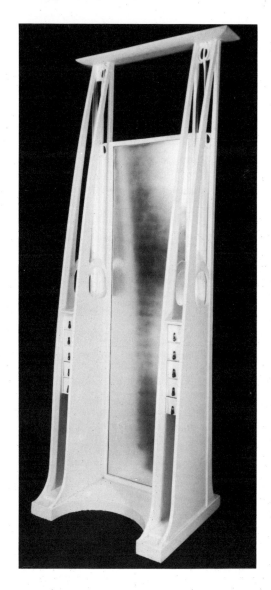

Right: Chair with high back for 120 Mains Street, Glasgow (oak, painted white). A white painted version of a chair designed for the Ingram Street Tea Rooms, Glasgow. This example, however, probably had inserts of coloured glass in the square cut-outs of the back splats. Hunterian Art Gallery, University of Glasgow. 1900.11.

contained almost as much furniture, including a four-poster bed, a large double wardrobe and a cheval mirror. The expressively modelled organic decoration on these pieces was offset by inlays of coloured glass and was much more fluid and sculptural than anything Mackintosh had designed to date. It formed the starting point for the elegant and sophisticated furniture for which Mackintosh became renowned in Europe.

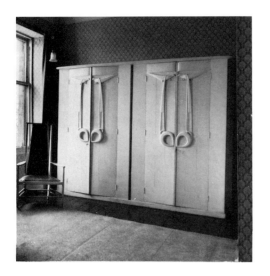

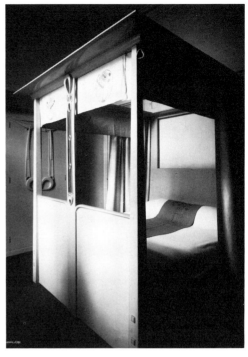

120 Mains Street, Glasgow. *Top left:* Double wardrobe (oak, painted white). A massive piece, decorated with high-relief carvings in the form of birds, originally inlaid with coloured glass or inserts of coloured paint. 1900.24. *Bottom left:* Bedroom table for 120 Mains Street, Glasgow (oak, painted white, with coloured glass inlay and white metal handle). Two were made to stand either side of the cheval mirror. 1900.27. *Right:* Four-poster bed (oak, painted white, with panels of coloured glass). The first of a number of four-poster beds that Mackintosh was to design. The carved decoration, of organic motifs, is particularly fine; the valances and curtains were all embroidered or stencilled with similar motifs. 1900.28. All Hunterian Art Gallery, University of Glasgow.

Mackintosh's work at Dunglass Castle, Bowling, for Margaret's father, Charles Macdonald, was probably slightly later than that in his own flat. It includes alterations to the drawing room fireplace and ceiling, as well as various pieces of furniture including a double bookcase, a four-poster bed and a cheval mirror.

Also in 1900, Mackintosh began work on another of Miss Cranston's Tea Rooms, at Ingram Street. This was the first job for her on which he had complete control over both furniture and decoration. The White Dining Room had the woodwork painted white and the movable furniture in dark-stained oak. It had a small mezzanine balcony, and kitchens, servery and Ladies' Dressing Room on the back (south) wall with access to the other

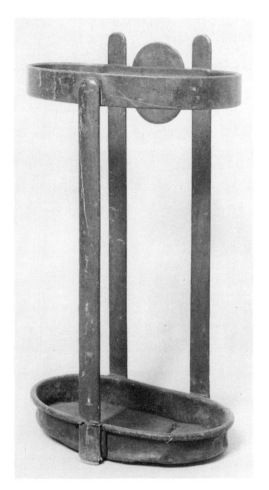

Left: Umbrella stand (lead over a steel frame). Probably designed around 1900 for use at 120 Mains Street, Glasgow. Hunterian Art Gallery, University of Glasgow. 1900.33.

Top right: Washstand for 120 Mains Street, Glasgow (oak, painted white). A simple design, the top of which was probably removed by Mackintosh when he moved to 78 Southpark Avenue in 1906. Hunterian Art Gallery, University of Glasgow. 1900.30.

Centre right: Washstand for 120 Mains Street, Glasgow (oak, stained dark, with black and white painted chequer decoration). Probably designed for use in a spare bedroom, where it would harmonise with the 1896 bed. Glasgow School of Art. 1900.31.

Bottom right: Hall settle (oak, stained dark). Probably designed around 1900 for use at 120 Mains Street, Glasgow. Hunterian Art Gallery, University of Glasgow. 1900.34.

tea rooms in the building. The main cash desk was accommodated under the stairs to the balcony. On the east and west walls were long gesso panels, *The Wassail* by Mackintosh and *The May Queen* by Margaret Macdonald. The billiards room, which had dark-stained panelling, was in the basement. At this stage, the only other room on which Mackintosh worked was the Cloister Room. A contemporary photograph shows stencilling and a screen

Dunglass Castle, Bowling. *Above:* Drawing room. This photograph was taken before Mackintosh carried out his alterations to the fireplace and ceiling in 1900. 1899.M. *Below:* Drawing room after the alterations had been carried out. Another of Mackintosh's imposing fireplaces. The decorations over the fireplace and on the settle are by the Macdonald sisters.

1900.A. *Opposite page. Below:* Bookcase for Dunglass Castle, Bowling (oak, painted white, with leaded glass doors). A version of the bookcase that Mackintosh designed for himself at 120 Mains Street, Glasgow, but with a simpler pattern in the doors. National Museum of Antiquities of Scotland, Edinburgh. 1900.38.

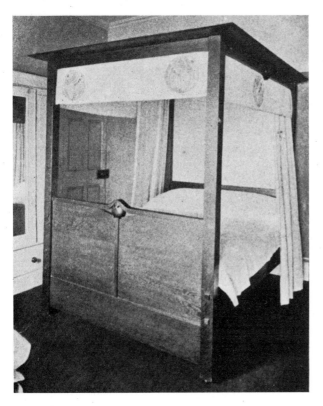

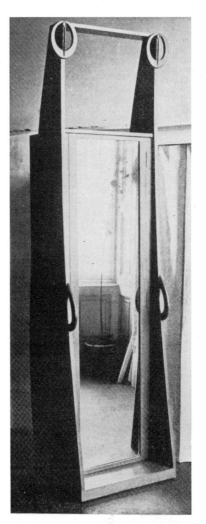

Left: Four-poster bed for Dunglass Castle, Bowling (wood, stained dark or ebonised). Untraced. 1900.40.
Right: Cheval mirror (wood, painted white). Possibly made for Dunglass Castle, Bowling, to accompany the bedroom furniture. Untraced. 1900.47.

Ingram Street Tea Rooms, Glasgow. *Above:* Balcony of the White Dining Room. The stylised stencilled tree on the wall was repeated around this small mezzanine balcony. The leaded glass casements screened a ventilation duct from the kitchens below. 1900.I.

Below: Billiards Room, with billiards table (untraced, 1900.72) made to Mackintosh's design by Burroughs & Watt and fitted seating (pine, stained dark, with upholstered seats and backs). 1900.J. Fitted seating, Glasgow Art Galleries and Museums, 1900.73.

Ingram Street Tea Rooms, Glasgow.
Above: The White Dining Room. This
contemporary photograph shows the layout of
the furniture, Mackintosh's large gesso panel,
The Wassail, and the original position of the
entrance screen (pine, painted white, with
panels of leaded glass). The screen channelled
patrons from the street door to the cash desk
and then through to the rest of the Tea Rooms.
1900.G. Screen, Glasgow Art Galleries and
Museums, 1900.66.

of Mackintosh's design, with furniture like that used in the White Dining
Room, but the original ornate plaster frieze was untouched. This scheme
was swept away in 1911 when the Cloister Room was totally redesigned.
Mackintosh did further work at the Ingram Street Tea Rooms from 1907,
after Miss Cranston had acquired the adjacent premises. The tea rooms
were dismantled in 1971 by the Planning Department of Glasgow Corporation and are now in the possession of Glasgow Art Galleries and Museums.
Much less is known about Ingram Street than about Miss Cranston's other
tea rooms, as no job-books survive for the project and there was no complete contemporary photographic survey like that of Mackintosh's next
work for Miss Cranston, the Willow Tea Rooms.

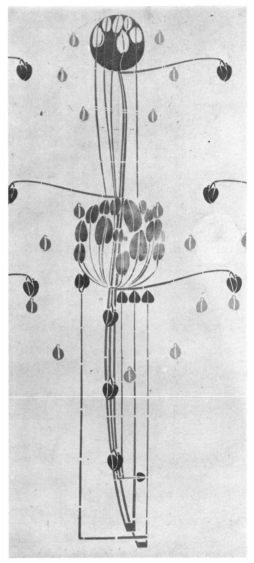

Ingram Street Tea Rooms, Glasgow.
Top left: The Cloister Room. A contemporary photograph showing how Mackintosh left untouched the ornate plaster ceiling and frieze. In 1911-12 he hid these behind a new barrel-vaulted ceiling, although he retained the open screen seen at the end of the room. 1900.K.

Bottom left: Umbrella stand (wrought iron). Probably made for the Ingram Street Tea Rooms but it may be earlier, possibly designed for use at the Argyle Street Tea Rooms, Glasgow. Glasgow Art Galleries and Museums; Glasgow School of Art. 1900.53.

Right: Stencil decoration in the Cloister Room. This elegant pattern was destroyed when Mackintosh remodelled the room in 1911-12. 1900.L.

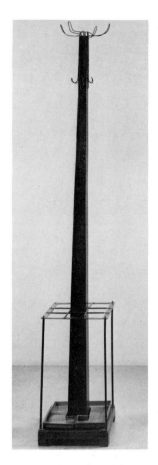 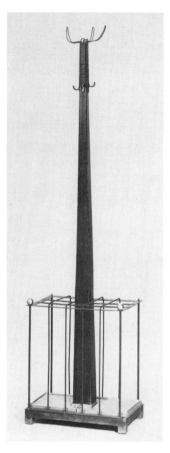 

Ingram Street Tea Rooms, Glasgow.
Top left: Hat, coat and umbrella stand for the
White Dining Room (oak and wrought iron).
1900.49.

Top centre: Hat, coat and umbrella stand for
the White Dining Room (oak and wrought
iron). 1900.50.

Top right: Display cabinet (pine, stained dark,
with glazed doors). The base of the glazed
section has a slatted shelf, beneath which the
top drawer is lined with metal. This drawer was
presumably intended to hold hot coals or ice for
warming or cooling food displayed in the upper
half of the cabinet. 1900.61.

Right: Serving table for the White Dining
Room, Ingram Street Tea Rooms, Glasgow
(pine, painted white). This appears to have
been the only piece of white-painted, free-
standing furniture designed for Ingram Street at
this date. The group of three squares echoes the
pattern in the tall chair for the same room.
1900.60. All Glasgow Art Galleries and
Museums.

63

Ingram Street Tea Rooms, Glasgow. *Top left:* Low chair for the White Dining Room, Ingram Street Tea Rooms, Glasgow (oak, stained dark, with horsehair upholstery). This chair is identical with the chairs from the dining room at Ingram Street except that the rear uprights

and splats have been shortened. This was probably done in 1912 when the Cloister Room was remodelled. Glasgow Art Galleries and Museums; Glasgow School of Art. 1900.56. *Top centre:* Chair for White Dining Room (oak, stained dark, with horsehair upholstery). The basic chair used in the main dining room and the Cloister Room in 1900. Glasgow Art Galleries and Museums; Glasgow School of Art; Hunterian Art Gallery, University of Glasgow. 1900.54. *Top right:* High-backed chair for the White Dining Room (oak, stained dark, with horsehair upholstery). A tall, elegant chair–the first high-backed design since 1897. Mackintosh kept one example for himself and painted it white for his flat at 120 Mains Street, Glasgow. Glasgow Art Galleries and Museums; Glasgow School of Art. 1900.55. *Left:* Fireplace for the White Dining Room (lead and coloured glass). A simple design incorporating motifs based on flowers in the applied panels of lead and glass. The grate is now missing but sketches show that it was a version of the wrought iron design in the drawing room at 120 Mains Street, Glasgow. Glasgow Art Galleries and Museums. 1900.62.

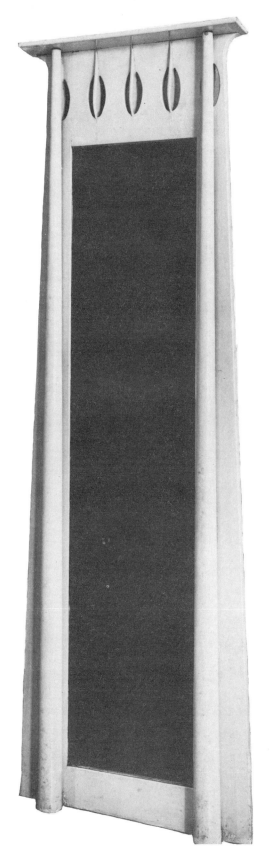

Ingram Street Tea Rooms, Glasgow. *Left:*
Mirror for the Ladies' Dressing Room (pine,
painted white). A simpler version of the full-
length mirrors designed for 120 Mains Street
(1900), Windyhill (1901) and The Hill House
(1903). Glasgow Art Galleries and Museums.
1900.70.
Top right: Billiards marker-board. Untraced.
1900.74. *Bottom right:* Umbrella stand (pine,
painted white). Possibly made for the Ingram
Street Tea Rooms, Glasgow. Glasgow School
of Art. 1900.76.

THE VIENNA SECESSION & THE HAUS EINES KUNSTFREUNDES, 1900-01

In July 1900, Carl Moll, President of the Vienna Secession, wrote to Mackintosh returning some photographs and requesting permission to publish some of them in the Secession magazine *Ver Sacrum*; it was perhaps in the same letter that he asked Mackintosh to contribute to the eighth exhibition of the Secession in the autumn of 1900. Mackintosh's flat had been photographed by Annan in March 1900, and prints of the interiors would almost certainly have been included in the parcel he sent to Vienna. In a letter to Moll on 17th December 1900, Mackintosh apologised for not returning the packet of photographs earlier as he had 'carefully put it away and I have been hunting for it ever since I came home' [from Vienna]. The photographs were published, along with views of Mackintosh's Secession room in *Ver Sacrum*, issue 23, 1901. These interiors would have had a profound effect upon the Secessionists, whose own work at that time did not display such precise control over the layout of interiors and furniture. Mackintosh's contribution to the eighth exhibition would no doubt have confirmed the promise of the earlier magazine articles, for his display was as particular and elegant as his own drawing room.

Mackintosh was given a substantial space, which he furnished sparsely with about ten pieces of furniture and a number of watercolours, mostly by Margaret and Frances Macdonald. The woodwork was painted white, with no wall decoration other than a series of tapered square posts, like those in his Mains Street dining room, attached to a deep horizontal wall-plate inset with square panels of coloured glass – a repetition of the motif in his own drawing room. But the most striking and perhaps the most influential feature of the design (apart from its overall elegance and restraint) was the inclusion of the two wide gesso panels designed and made by Mackintosh and Margaret Macdonald for the White Room at the Ingram Street Tea Rooms. These were placed at a

Opposite page. Above: Room at the Eighth Exhibition of the Vienna Secession. This photograph shows Mackintosh's large gesso panel, *The Wassail*, and some of the furniture and watercolours exhibited at Vienna; also a flower stand (untraced, 1900.79), the simple design being an enlargement of the ceramic or metal flower vases used at 120 Mains Street, Glasgow. 1900.M. *Below left:* Fireplace for the Eighth Exhibition of the Vienna Secession. An extremely plain, simple structure containing no grate. The fire-screen in front of it is a beaten metal panel designed and made by Margaret Macdonald. Fireplace untraced; panel, Hunterian Art Gallery, University of Glasgow. 1900.77. *Below right:* Sideboard/cabinet (oak, with leaded glass and beaten metal panels). The metal panels were made by Margaret and the leaded glass is a variant of the pieces used in the screen at the Ingram Street Tea Rooms, Glasgow. In 1902 the cabinet was painted white and was shown at Turin, where it was bought by a Viennese collector. Untraced. 1900.78.

Room at the Eighth Exhibition of the Vienna Secession. The gesso panel on the wall is Margaret Macdonald's *The May Queen*. The clock and the embroidered panel are by her and her sister, Frances. 1900.N.

high level, above the deep picture rail, anticipating the gesso panels to be designed for Wärndorfer's music room in 1902. This creation of a deep decorative frieze was to have a profound effect on Gustav Klimt, who must surely have been influenced by it in his own exhibit for the fourteenth Secession exhibition, the *Beethoven Frieze*.

The effect of the room at the Secession can be seen in the design contributions to later exhibitions from Josef Hoffmann and his colleagues. Many of the earlier Secession exhibitions had been cluttered and poorly presented, notwithstanding the clear lines and adaptable spaces which J.M. Olbrich's superb building gave the exhibitors. With the exception of the clock by Margaret and Frances Macdonald, all the furniture was of Mackintosh's design, although he seems to have made no new pieces specifically for the exhibition room, apart from the door and the fireplace – the large cabinet might have been a speculative piece, as was the settle shown at the Arts & Crafts Exhibition Society in 1896. This cabinet was a variant on the large desk that Mackintosh had made for his own flat; it was typical of the period, with beaten metal panels designed by Margaret Macdonald. The cabinet was not sold until it was sent to Turin in 1902, sporting a coat of white paint (when Wärndorfer appears to have bought it). The only pieces that remained in Vienna were an oval back-rail armchair acquired by Kolo Moser, who later became a good friend of Mackintosh, and Mackintosh's own smoker's cabinet, which was bought by Hugo Henneberg and fitted into a study in a house being designed for him by Hoffmann.

Mackintosh's work had a profound influence upon the younger Viennese designers. Even Hoffmann assimilated some of his ideas, but it was his students who were most impressed by the work of the Scottish architect. The style they evolved bore little resemblance to the pieces that Mackintosh had actually exhibited in Vienna, but a growing dependence on white paint, coloured inlays and the use of the square as a decorative motif points to a considerable knowledge of other pieces designed by Mackintosh which were not shown at Vienna in 1900. Obviously he had sent quite a number of photographs to Moll in the summer of 1900, and he probably took more with him when he visited Vienna with Margaret in October or November that year. After that, his work received much more publicity in the German art periodicals, and Mackintosh was himself in correspondence with Moser, Hoffmann and Wärndorfer, all of whom would have known of his plans and dreams.

After 1900, the aims of Mackintosh and the Viennese designers were similar, and I believe that the increasing appearance of geometrical motifs in the Secessionists' designs was inspired by Mackintosh. A popular Viennese motif was a group of four pierced or incised squares; this had been used by Mackintosh at Westdel as early as 1898, and single squares appear on the Ingram Street furniture and in the picture rails both at Mains Street and at the Secession display. Lattice panelling, another Secession motif, had been used by Mackintosh in an exhibition stand for the School of Art early in 1901 and was implicit in the mullions and transoms of the School of Art studio windows, completed in 1899. While the Viennese eventually used the square, the oblong, the lattice and the triangle in an excessively mannered way, Mackintosh continued to explore the challenge of integrating organic decoration into his furniture while continuing to work along a parallel course with more geometrical motifs. The latter eventually came to dominate his work, but from 1900 to 1903 he concentrated on the white-painted, almost symbolist furniture on which much of his fame as a designer rests.

The exhibition was an enormous critical success for Mackintosh and forged links with men like Hoffmann, Klimt, Moser and Wärndorfer. Few direct commissions, however, seem to have arisen out of the exhibition, for, with the exception of the music room for Wärndorfer in 1902, the only other work that Mackintosh did in Europe was connected with competitions and exhibition rooms. There can be little doubt, though, that the exhibition brought other rewards, as it introduced Mackintosh's work to a generation of Viennese designers and students who were to emulate his designs for years to come. It also put him in the limelight as one of the leading British designers and architects: in future years, the publishers of the German art periodicals, *Dekorative Kunst* and *Deutsche Kunst und Dekoration*, devoted more space to his work

Top left: Cabinet for Michael Diack (oak, stained dark, with glazed doors). Diack was a musician and publisher for whom Mackintosh designed a number of items. 1900.81. *Top right:* Detail of cabinet. 1900.81. *Below:* Writing desk for Michael Diack (oak, stained dark, with panels of leaded glass and metal). The desk incorporates a fine decorative panel in the form of a weeping rose, the first appearance of a motif to be used many times in later desks and cabinets. 1901.1.

than to that of any of his British contemporaries (save, perhaps, Baillie Scott), thus providing him with the acclaim that the British press denied him.

The competition to design a house for a connoisseur of the arts was announced in the December 1900 issue of *Zeitschrift für Innendekoration*, published by Alexander Koch in Darmstadt. It seems reasonable to assume that Mackintosh would have heard about the competition on his visit to Vienna, where it would almost certainly have been a topic of discussion among the architects and designers he met at the Secession, especially as J.M. Olbrich was one of the judges. The closing date was 25th March 1901 and the adjudication was set for 16th and 17th May in Darmstadt. Mackintosh's entry was initially disqualified because he did not submit the required number of interior perspectives; after he had prepared these, his drawings were awarded the purchase prize of 600 marks and reproduced in one of the folios of competition drawings that were

Above: Elevation of the south wall of the hall, *Haus eines Kunstfreundes*. A two-storeyed room, like the museum at Queen Margaret Medical College (1895). The pendants on the gallery balustrade are reminiscent of those at Queen's Cross Church. 1901.4. *Below:* Perspective of the dining room, *Haus eines Kunstfreundes*. The most elaborate dining room Mackintosh had designed to date. He has retained his favoured arrangement of dark walls and furniture but the whole composition is lightened by the extensive use of stencilled panels on the walls and cupboards. 1901.6.

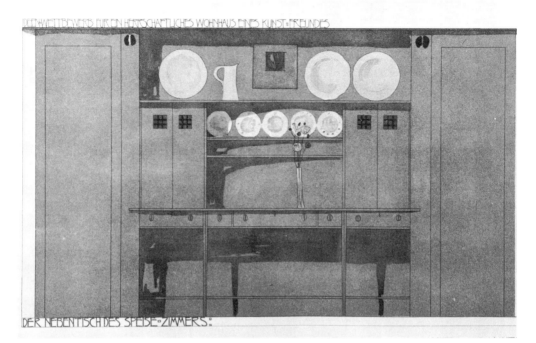

DER NEBENTISCH DES SPEISE=ZIMMERS:

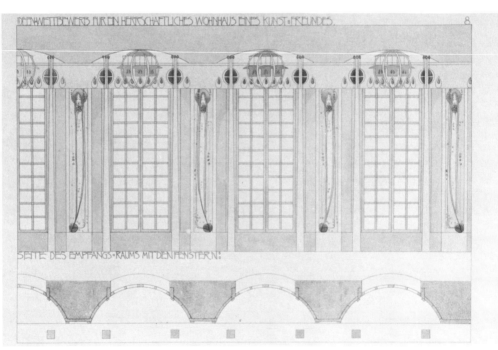

SEITE DES EMPFANGS=RAUMS MIT DEN FENSTERN:

issued in 1902 under the title *Meister der Innenkunst*. There was no first prize awarded, the prize money being divided between more than sixteen competitors. The second prize was given to M.H. Baillie Scott, and the third was shared by Leopold Bauer and Oskar Marmorek of Vienna and Paul Zeroch of Coblenz. My concern here is with the interiors of the house. The judges were most impressed by the interior planning of Baillie Scott's design, but they felt that his exteriors and massing were not 'modern', nor as accomplished as those

Right: Elevations of the drawing room fireplace and the music room piano for the *Haus eines Kunstfreundes*. The piano, with its fantastic superstructure, is based on the organ made for Craigie Hall, Glasgow, in 1897. 1901.8.

Opposite page. Above: Elevation of the sideboard in the dining room. 1901.5. *Below:* Elevation of the windows in the drawing room of the *Haus eines Kunstfreundes*. 1901.7.

Below: Elevation of a bedroom wall for the *Haus eines Kunstfreundes*. Many of the features seen here were also used in the main bedroom at Windyhill in 1901. 1901.10.

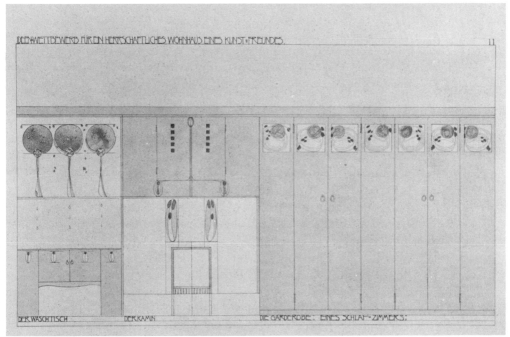

by Mackintosh, whose interiors were more carefully controlled but less spatially exciting. As Mackintosh never built a house on this scale, the plans and interior schemes are worth examining in some detail.

As at Windyhill, one would enter from the north and turn through 90° into the dark-stained hall. Here the hall has two stories, with a gallery corridor linking the bedrooms and with full height windows to the north. From the hall, a corridor leads to the study, an oval room for the ladies and a smoking room

EMPFANGS··RAUM ii MUSIK··ZIMMER PANELS von MARGARET MACDONALD MACKINTOSH

Above: Perspective of the drawing and music rooms, *Haus eines Kunstfreundes*. A stunning composition in white, silver, pink, purple and green where Margaret Macdonald's specific talents are skilfully used to produce a harmonious blend of the functional and the decorative. 1901.9. *Opposite page:* Perspective of the schoolroom, *Haus eines Kunstfreundes*. The furniture is all loosely based on Mackintosh's designs for nursery furniture at Gladsmuir. The gesso panel over the fireplace was to have been made by Margaret. 1901.11.

for the gentlemen. To the west lie the dining room and a morning room; a movable partition allows the dining room and hall to be used as a single room 20 metres long. To the south, doors beneath the gallery lead to the drawing and music rooms; these can also be used as one room of 16 × 5 metres.

The main staircase has an apsidal outer wall, like those Mackintosh was to design for Windyhill and The Hill House, and rises in two flights to the first floor. (A second staircase connects the service rooms in the basement with all the upper floors.) Again as at Windyhill and The Hill House, the bedrooms lead off a central corridor, which becomes an open gallery as it passes through the hall. The main bedroom, which has its own bathroom, is isolated at one end of the house and insulated from the other rooms by a door across the corridor; a guests' sitting room is placed between it and the next room, a guest room. The children's rooms are at the far end of the corridor, as is the breakfast room with its bow window (a feature repeated at The Hill House). The schoolroom is on the attic floor above the children's bedrooms. These specific arrangements appeared two years later at The Hill House and have often been attributed to the brief from the client, Walter Blackie.

In two rooms of the *Haus eines Kunstfreundes*, the bedroom and the combined music and reception room, Mackintosh made extensive use of white

DER SPIEL∘∘RAUM DER KINDER   PANEL von MARGARET MACDONALD MACKINTOSH□

paint. Only one drawing appears to have been made of a bedroom, the south-facing main bedroom, which has a number of features that are worth noting as they reappear at The Hill House of 1902-03. The single elevation shown in Mackintosh's competition design is very different from the Mains Street bedroom, and more like the fireplace wall of the Headmaster's room at the Glasgow School of Art in treatment. The row of simple fitted wardrobes is painted and embellished with stencilled squares. The beds are screened from the rest of the room in an alcove, from which there is access to a dressing room; at the opposite end of the room is a fireplace with fireside chairs and above it a medicine cupboard decorated with pierced squares. The washstand is very similar to the simple rectilinear shapes produced for the Dunglass bedroom, and no other furniture is shown. As the arrangement of the room was repeated in the Windyhill bedroom of 1901, it seems likely that, if the *Haus eines Kunstfreundes* had been built, the movable furniture would have been similar to that for Windyhill.

The music and reception room was the most ornate room that Mackintosh had so far designed, for, although the furniture is sparsely distributed, the walls, especially the east and west walls, are by his standards extremely elaborate. The south wall is broken by a series of shallow, curved window bays, each containing a tall stencilled or embroidered panel designed by Margaret Macdonald. At the west end of the room is a piano or organ, above which is suspended one of the most elaborate of Mackintosh's decorative sculptures, which combines motifs of birds, trees and flowers, an elaboration of the Craigie Hall organ of 1897. At the other end of the room, the fireplace, again with ornate applied decoration, is flanked by two cabinets supported on spindly legs; these faced two large figurative panels flanking the piano/organ on the west wall. The whole treatment of the room, with its crisp white furniture offset by tints of rose, purple and green in the light shades and inlays, was much more consciously elegant than anything Mackintosh had previously designed. Apart from the panels that were actually designed by Margaret, the entire room reflects her influence, or at least a more feminine point of view than is apparent in the rest of the designs for the house. It was the music room that attracted the most attention of all the interior views and almost certainly inspired Wärndorfer to ask Mackintosh to design the music room for his own house. That room, as finally executed with its frieze of gesso panels, is very close to the *Haus eines Kunstfreundes* design and is the apogee, and virtually the final example, of Mackintosh's work in this new style.

At Windyhill there is little of this style to be seen, and even the white bed-room is somewhat severe. In the series of designs for stalls for the Glasgow International Exhibition of 1901, however, the two extremes of Mackintosh's style can be seen: the rigid white lattice-work of the School of Art kiosk stands in stark contrast to the more curvilinear designs for Pettigrew & Stephens, the Rae Brothers, or Francis Smith, which come closest to the extravagant piano/organ proposed for the *Haus eines Kunstfreundes* earlier in the year.

Exhibition stand for Pettigrew & Stephens for the Glasgow International Exhibition, 1901. The heavy carving over the stand is perhaps a little coarse and this seems the least successful of the various stands Mackintosh was to design for this Exhibition. Untraced. 1901.20.

Francis Smith operated a cabinetmaking, joinery and decorating business in Glasgow and made much of Mackintosh's furniture after 1900. Untraced. 1901.22. *Below:* Exhibition stand for Messrs. Rae Brothers at the Glasgow International Exhibition, 1901. The most elaborate of the four stands at the Exhibition. The posts along the front of the stand are white-painted replicas of those in the dining-room at Mains Street and the cabinet inside the stand is very similar to the writing desk shown at Turin in 1902. Untraced. 1901.24.

Left: Exhibition stand for the Glasgow School of Art at the Glasgow International Exhibition, 1901. A basic cube in shape, Mackintosh has developed his design around a theme of the lattice, contrasting open against closed squares in the structure. Untraced. 1901.21. *Right:* Exhibition stand for Francis Smith at the Glasgow International Exhibition, 1901.

Windyhill, Kilmacolm. *Above:* The hall. A dual purpose room – it also served as a dining room for large family parties. The fireplace (*in situ*, 1901.34) has no elaborate surround as in most other designs but a simple flat plate attached to the wall, framing the grate. The two posts repeat the arrangement in the dining room at 120 Mains Street, Glasgow. T.& R. Annan, Glasgow. 1901.A. *Below:* The hall and staircase. T.& R. Annan, Glasgow. 1901.B.

WINDYHILL & KINGSBOROUGH GARDENS 1901-02

Mackintosh designed Windyhill at Kilmacolm around 1900 for William Davidson Jr, who had known him for about five years and already owned several pieces of furniture designed by him, some of them specially commissioned for Davidson's parents' house, Gladsmuir. All this furniture seems to have been taken to Windyhill along with other items not designed by Mackintosh. In 1901, Davidson was in correspondence with Mackintosh about new furniture for Windyhill, although there never seems to have been any intention of furnishing the house entirely with pieces designed by the architect.

The new movable furniture was confined to the hall, drawing room, playroom and main bedroom. The hall served as the family dining room for large gatherings, and existing dining furniture was presumably placed in the small dining room. The wood used throughout in the new furniture was oak, usually stained and polished, with the exception of the main bedroom where it was painted white. The woodwork and decorations in the house followed the same general pattern as at 120 Mains Street. The hall has a broad plate in place of a conventional picture rail, with the walls below it divided into wide panels by similar vertical straps. All this timber, including the doors and skirtings, is stained dark, and the whole of the dining room is panelled with dark-stained timber to a height of about 2.2 metres.

The drawing room has a white fireplace and white-painted woodwork around the window, but no timber panelling or strapwork. One wall of the drawing room – the west wall – seems to have been papered in a dark colour with a white frieze above, in a style similar to that of the Mains Street dining room. All the other walls, however, seem to have been one colour from skirting to ceiling.

The staircase was broad and well-lit and the walls were panelled to level with the top of the last tread, with the central panel between the flights extending higher than the wall panelling to form an L-shaped balustrade with alternate boards removed and coloured glass squares inserted into those that remained. As at the School of Art, there was no handrail; a single, tapering, square newel post reaches to a simple, square 'capital' fixed to the ceiling. The main bedroom is painted white and decorated with stencils.

The drawing room window, Windyhill, Kilmacolm. The early desk, made for Gladsmuir, can be clearly seen; in the foregound is the tea table, now lost. T.& R. Annan, Glasgow. 1901.D.

Bookcase in the drawing room, Windyhill, Kilmacolm. This contemporary photograph shows that Mackintosh applied a dark paper to the west wall of the room. T.& R. Annan, Glasgow. 1901.E.

The dining room, Windyhill, Kilmacolm. Mackintosh juxtaposed the chair he designed for the hall with a traditional 'Orkney' chair belonging to the Davidsons. The room is dark, like all Mackintosh's dining rooms, but it is panelled rather than wall-papered. No furniture was designed specifically for the room. T.& R. Annan, Glasgow. 1901.F.

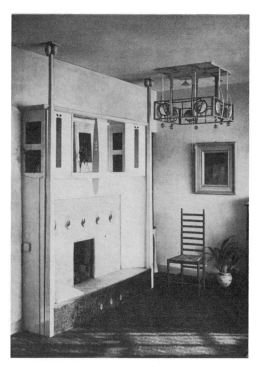

Top left: The drawing room, Windyhill, Kilmacolm. This contemporary photograph shows the original fireplace (now destroyed) and one of the light fittings. The fireplace (wood, painted white) was a more complex and elaborate composition than those at Mains Street or Dunglass of 1900. T.& R. Annan, Glasgow. 1901.C. Fireplace, 1901.35. *Top right:* The staircase, Windyhill, Kilmacolm.

T.& R. Annan, Glasgow. 1901.H. *Below:* Bedroom, Windyhill, Kilmacolm. The only contemporary photograph to show the arrangement of the fitted furniture (oak, painted white with stencilled decoration) on the west wall, which was very similar to that in the *Haus eines Kunstfreundes*. T.& R. Annan, Glasgow. 1901.I. Fitted furniture, *in situ*, 1901.45.

timber used for the top. To accommodate extra diners, Mackintosh designed a small extension table which was placed at one end. 1901.26.

Top right: Extension table for the hall (oak, stained green). 1901.27. Both Glasgow School of Art.

Left: Chair with high tapering back for the hall (oak, stained dark). One of the most striking, and certainly one of the sturdiest, of Mackintosh's designs for chairs. Hunterian Art Gallery, University of Glasgow. 1901.31.

Above: Bench for the hall (oak, stained green). A very simple design which was used alongside the long table instead of chairs. 1901.29. Glasgow School of Art.

Windyhill, Kilmacolm. *Top left:* Hall table (oak, stained green). The design is simple, the solid legs contrasting with the thin planks of

The lighting in the house was far more elaborate than that at Mains Street, where the fittings were simply a development of those used for the Buchanan Street and Argyle Street Tea Rooms. As the fuel used was gas, the fittings were open to allow the easy passage of air and fumes. The hall lanterns were simple squares of glass; brackets were used in the dining room and the main bedroom. The fittings for the staircase and the drawing room, however, used patterns of leaded glass and wrought iron, with hanging glass plaques and glass balls for decoration.

Windyhill, Kilmacolm. *Above:*
Bookcase (oak, stained dark, with leaded-glass panels). A fine piece of furniture, developed from sketches for a toy chest for the school room. Glasgow School of Art. 1901.38. *Left:* Fireplace (pine, stained dark) in the dining room. *In situ.* 1901.42. *Right:* Washstand for the main bedroom (oak, painted white). Like much of the Windyhill bedroom furniture, this piece was based on a design in the *Haus eines Kunstfreundes* competition. Glasgow School of Art. 1901.44.

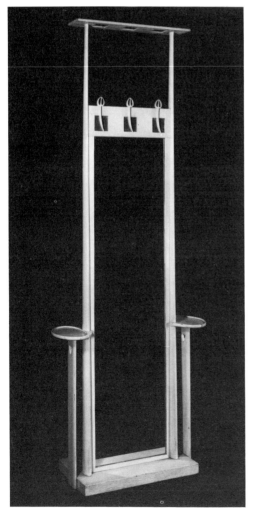

Windyhill, Kilmacolm. *Top left:* Table for the main bedroom (oak, painted white). Other tables like this, but stained dark, were made for the children's bedrooms. Hunterian Art Gallery, University of Glasgow. 1901.47.

Bottom left: Cheval mirror for the main bedroom (oak, painted white). A less elaborate design than that for 120 Mains Street, Glasgow. Glasgow School of Art. 1901.49.

Right: Ladderback chair (oak). A more elegant response to a traditional design than some of the early tea room ladderbacks. Glasgow School of Art. 1901.52.

Opposite page. Top: Bed (oak, painted white). A heavy, solid piece, its broad areas of white paint broken only by the high relief of the sculptural decoration. Glasgow School of Art. 1901.51.

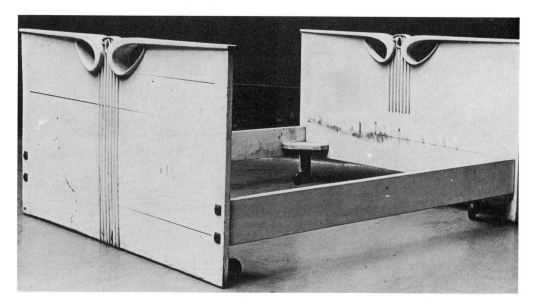

Above: Fender for 3 Lilybank Terrace, Glasgow (only the fender, in steel, glass and leather, survives). The fender was for a large, white-painted fireplace, which originally incorporated a decorative gesso panel by Margaret Macdonald. Glasgow School of Art. 1901.57.

In the following year, 1902, Mackintosh had the opportunity to put into practice some of the ideas already seen in his *Haus eines Kunstfreundes* designs. At the end of 1901, he was invited to undertake some work for Mrs Rowat, mother of Fra Newbery's wife, Jessie, at 14 (now 34) Kingsborough Gardens, Glasgow, which is a quiet street of large terraced houses overlooking a private garden in the west of Glasgow. He was to decorate several rooms and remodel the dining room fireplace. The elaborate fittings and wall decorations were designed late in 1901, and were complemented by pieces of furniture made specifically for the house over a period of a few months at the beginning of 1902; most of the pieces were probably not designed and possibly not even commissioned until after the completion of the decorations, although there is insufficient documentary evidence to allow an accurate dating of the work at Kingsborough Gardens.

The drawing room is completely different in feeling from anything in Mains Street or even Windyhill. The major change in style is the introduction of an overall pattern of stencilling on the walls and the repetition of a stencilled design on the backs of the fitted seats. At Mains Street, the emphasis had been on simplicity, and none of the walls had such an overall, rather fussy pattern; even at Windyhill, stencilling was used only in the bedrooms. After the carefully controlled interiors of Mains Street, the

14 Kingsborough Gardens, Glasgow. *Above:*
Drawing room with fitted settles (painted
white, with upholstered seats and stencilled
backs) and fireplace (wood, painted white, with
inlaid glass decoration). The carved and pierced
motifs in the woodwork were repeated on
several of the items of furniture designed for
the room. Drawing room, 1902.A. Settles,
destroyed, 1901.60. Fireplace, *in situ*, 1901.59.

Left: Oval table (oak, painted white, with two
inlaid ivory panels). A design which pleased
Mackintosh – he repeated it for his own use
and also incorporated it in later exhibition
stands. Hunterian Art Gallery, University of
Glasgow. 1902.1.

Below: Cabinet. 1902.3. *See opposite page for
caption.*

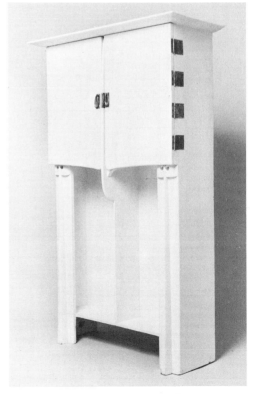

Top: Cabinets in the drawing room, 14
Kingsborough Gardens, Glasgow. 1902.B.
Centre: Cabinets at 120 Mains Street, Glasgow.
A contemporary photograph of Mackintosh's
own version of the cabinets for 14
Kingsborough Gardens. 1902.C. *Left:* Cabinet,
with inlaid glass panels inside the doors, for 14
Kingsborough Gardens, Glasgow (oak, painted
white; insides of doors silvered and inlaid with
coloured glass; white metal hinges and
handles). A design with a jewel-like
preciousness achieved by the combination of
the purple glass, the silver leaf and the white
paint. Two cabinets were made for
Kingsborough Gardens and Mackintosh made
two for himself. Hunterian Art Gallery,
University of Glasgow; Royal Ontario
Museum, Toronto. 1902.3.

decorations at Kingsborough Gardens come as a shock and might be considered a retrograde step; certainly the effect is less stark, almost less modern, and it brings with it a change in furniture design.

Most of the pieces for Windyhill are in the robust style that can be traced back to the designs for the Argyle Street Tea Rooms: they are fairly solid, with broad expanses of timber and occasional decoration of *repoussé* metal, glass, or carved wood. In character, they are strongly architectural, and even the white-painted bedroom furniture has little romance about it. Kingsborough Gardens, on the other hand, with its patterns of stylised flowers and delicate white-painted furniture, belongs firmly to the group of work from 1901-03 in which Margaret seems to have played an identifiable part – the *Haus eines Kunstfreundes* music room, the Rose Boudoir for the Turin Exhibition, the Wärndorfer music salon and the room at the Moscow Exhibition of 1903. The elegant armchairs, with their spindly legs and stretchers, and the subtle curves of the oval table are so different from the hall furniture for Windyhill that one might be forgiven for believing them to be the work of a different artist. The two cabinets, with an internal glass inlay on each door in the shape of a girl holding a rose-ball, betray Margaret's influence as clearly as the writing desk shown at the Turin Exhibition.

Left: Armchair with leather or velvet upholstery for 14 Kingsborough Gardens, Glasgow (oak, painted white). An elegant design, upholstered in purple velvet at Kingsborough Gardens, but in leather in this example, which Mackintosh kept for himself. This chair is the first of a series of pieces of a more delicate form and structure. Hunterian Art Gallery, University of Glasgow. 1902.2.

Right: Hall settle for 14 Kingsborough Gardens, Glasgow (oak, stained dark). A bold, masculine design relating more to the hall furniture at Windyhill than to the white-painted furniture in the drawing room. *In situ.* 1901.62.

THE TURIN EXHIBITION & THE WÄRNDORFER MUSIC SALON, 1902

Several commentators have seen the influence of Margaret Macdonald in the tea room interiors, particularly the Willow, which was designed in 1903. While I would not deny that Margaret worked with her husband on that project, I believe that the most productive period of their joint work was concentrated in the years 1901-02. Margaret's fairy-tale world of myth and legend, of princesses being rescued by gallant knights (seen in her over-pretty post-1898 style), and her fascination with Arthurian legend and the stories of Maurice Maeterlinck are reflected in the interiors of 1902.

Fra Newbery, Headmaster of the Glasgow School of Art, was responsible for choosing the exhibits for the Scottish section of the International Exhibition of Modern Decorative Art at Turin in 1902. Not surprisingly, Newbery included very little work that did not originate from his own School; as designer of the stalls and room settings in his area he chose Mackintosh.

The two visited Turin, probably in April 1902, when Wärndorfer met Mackintosh and reported their discussions to Hoffmann. The specially constructed exhibition building designed by d'Aronco did not please Mackintosh: Wärndorfer quotes to Hoffmann his belief that it was 'the basest and meanest theft from what Olbrich did at Darmstadt'. Mackintosh broke up the Scottish area into three units. The gallery was much too high for his needs, and the windows too large. He solved these problems by the use of white paint on the ceiling and on the walls above about 2.5 metres; he softened the light by filtering it through a thin, muslin-like fabric. The apartments in the exhibit were linked together by a series of stencilled banners 4.5 metres high which bore the motif of a draped figure with her head silhouetted against the moon and her gown festooned with roses. The first bay, known as the Rose Boudoir, was designed to house furniture and paintings by the Mackintoshes; it was painted white, silver and rose-pink. The second bay was occupied by Margaret's sister, Frances MacNair, and her husband, Herbert. They decorated it as a writing room; it was painted grey, gold and white, relieved by a MacNair frieze in pink and green. The third unit was used to house the work of students from the Glasgow School of Art and the other Scottish exhibitors; it was the largest of the three and was painted purple and white. This division of the vast and somewhat unsympathetic space set the whole tone of the Scottish exhibit. Mackintosh

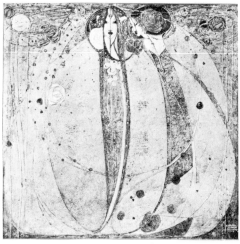

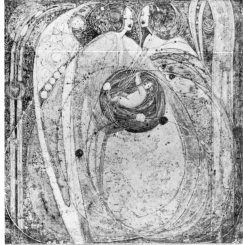

Above: The Scottish Exhibition area, International Exhibition of Decorative Art, Turin. The display cabinet (wood, painted white) is a small version of the stand designed by Mackintosh for the Glasgow International Exhibition of 1901. The banners (linen, stencilled in green, silver, rose and black) were used to break up the high space allocated to the Scottish designers and to divide the three individual bays which Mackintosh created. 1902.F. Display cabinet, 1902.5. Banner, Hunterian Art Gallery, University of Glasgow, 1902.6.

Below: Two gesso panels by Margaret Macdonald, *The White Rose and the Red Rose*

and *Heart of the Rose*, that hung at opposite ends of the Rose Boudoir at the Turin Exhibition. 1902.D.

Opposite page. Above: Two views of the writing desk for the International Exhibition of Decorative Art, Turin (ebonised wood with panels of metal and glass, and gesso designed by Margaret Macdonald Mackintosh). The most elaborate of the various writing cabinets designed by Mackintosh. The use of the gesso panels is not found on any other similar piece; their theme is the rose, to match the other gesso panels shown at Turin. The cabinet was bought by Fritz Wärndorfer for his Vienna house. Museum für Angewandte Kunst, Vienna. 1902.8.

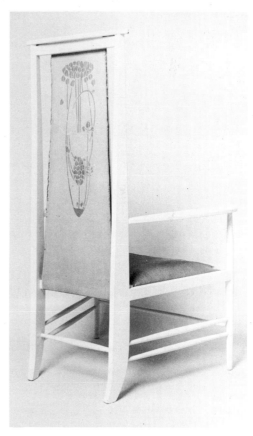

Left: The Rose Boudoir, International Exhibition of Decorative Arts, Turin. 1902.E. *Right:* Armchair with stencilled loose canvas back (oak, painted white, with upholstered seat). A variant of the Kingsborough Gardens chair but, instead of a solid upholstered back, Mackintosh has stretched a double sheet of canvas between top-rail and seat. This is stencilled with a floral motif, part of the Rose Boudoir theme. Hunterian Art Gallery, University of Glasgow. 1902.7.

wanted the structure to stand in its own right as part of the Scottish contribution; with his stencilled banners, the tall, tapering square posts and the unmoulded timber he easily achieved his aim.

Newbery's file on the Turin Exhibition is still preserved at the Glasgow School of Art and shows that, as with so many large exhibitions of this type, not everything went as well as had been expected, and the Scottish Committee eventually made a financial loss. The Mackintoshes, at least, confirmed their artistic reputations. Although several things remained unsold, they were invited to exhibit in Budapest and Moscow, and their work was awarded a diploma of honour.

Several new pieces of furniture were made specially for the Rose Boudoir. The walls were hung with small watercolours and beaten metal panels, but the most important pictures were, in fact, the gesso panels designed and made by Margaret around the theme of the rose. The stencils at Kingsborough Gardens had also used roses; at the Wärndorfer salon of 1902, the same year as the Turin Exhibition, Margaret's influence can be seen not only in the decoration of the furniture but also in the frieze of gesso panels based on Maeterlinck's *Seven Princesses* which again made much of the rose motif. In the Rose Boudoir, the backs of the chairs were stencilled with roses, and the colour scheme of pink, purple, green and white echoed that of the drawing room at Kingsborough Gardens.

I do not believe that Margaret played a direct part in designing the furniture for any of these rooms. Her part was in the choice of the decorations and in the emphasis on the creation of a fairy-tale or romantic setting for the furniture. The influence undoubtedly percolated through to the furniture itself, in that Mackintosh designed it to be in keeping with the mood of the room, but the physical design was surely his. Margaret never showed any real flair for working in three dimensions – her work was basically flat and linear. The only piece of furniture attributed to her, a three-cornered cabinet given by W. Davidson to Queen's Cross Church, is of uncertain, even clumsy, design.

The importance of the more romantic and feminine designs lies in the methods that Mackintosh used to break with the robust style of much of his earlier furniture. At Westdel, he had discovered that paint in itself helped to create elements of a new style: it freed him from the accepted associations of timber, the emphasis on grain and on traditional cabinet-making construction and decoration. The new furniture was painted white, not just to reinforce the concept of the unified interior, but also to conceal and deny the construction of the pieces themselves. The delicate legs and stretchers of the chairs, the wide legs of the tables, often placed tangentially to circular or oval tops and shelves, all provided insufficient contact to make good joints. The decoration of these structural and even non-structural members was often of a kind alien to the nature of wood. Had the timber been exposed, all the faults, as the Arts & Crafts designers would have called them, would have been exposed as well, and they would, at the very least, have detracted from the design. At worst, they would have destroyed it. To overcome this, Mackintosh gave his new designs a coat of icy white enamel, applied over a filler that obliterated all trace of the grain below.

He would probably have preferred to use a totally new material, something that was not expected to conform to accepted and well-tried rules of design and construction. Mackintosh saw no virtue in the use of materials for their own sake – the distortions of form and structure applied to the timber of these designs shows that where there was no aesthetic value to be

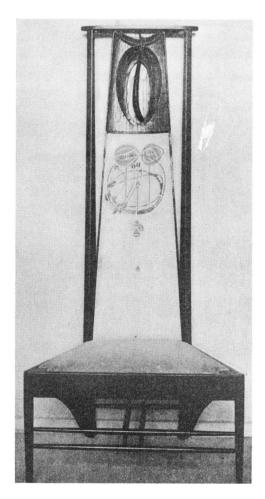
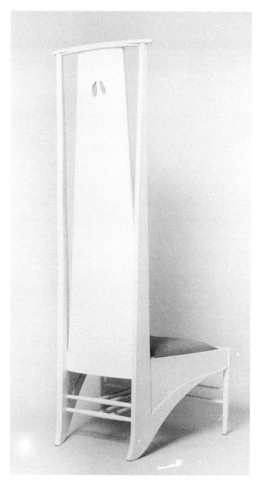

International Exhibition of Decorative Arts, Turin. *Left:* Chair with stencilled high back (oak, perhaps ebonised, with upholstered seat and back). Probably designed to accompany the desk. It was not bought by Wärndorfer, who commissioned the white-painted version of the chair for his Music Salon in Vienna. Untraced. 1902.11.

Right: Chair with stencilled high back (oak, painted white, with upholstered seat and back). Identical, except for its colour, to the other Turin chair. This one appears to have returned to Glasgow – a fortunate chance as all of the other similar chairs designed for Wärndorfer are now lost. Hunterian Art Gallery, University of Glasgow. 1902.12.

gained from the material he would pragmatically hide it; where it had a contribution to make, it would just as emphatically be exposed. There was, however, no other material available, and Mackintosh therefore had to transform wood. By painting it white, black or occasionally silver, he was able to release it from its traditional restrictions: it could be carved and planed in new ways which could be made acceptable by the homogeneity of the surface; joints and sections are visually (if not structurally) acceptable because the hard-painted surface suggests that they are not made of wood, which has structural limitations that we understand and accept, but of some elegant new substance.

After two or three years of frenetic experimentation with painted and carved surfaces, Mackintosh gave them up and returned to a more traditional use of timber for his furniture. This development was coupled with a rejection of the literal use of organic decoration in his work, but was also connected with his failure to produce furniture that had the structural strength of the earlier pieces. It is a fact that the most delicate of his pieces were produced between 1899 and 1903; they were painted and all more or less in the same style. It remains open to question whether Mackintosh painted his furniture to help conceal the structural inadequacies forced on him by the demands of style or whether he really did wish to create the illusion of using a new and as yet non-existent material.

During the years when Mackintosh was working closely with Margaret, his approach to the problems of furniture and interior design became less experimental. White furniture and white walls, with organic decoration on both, was a simplistic solution, as limited as Margaret's imagery in her watercolours and gesso panels. It restricted the architectural control of his interior spaces and gave designs an over-refined sophistication that would all too soon have become mannered and sterile. Without an alternative to wood, even Mackintosh's inventive powers would soon have become exhausted, for there was a limit to the distortion he could impose on his raw materials. In the two years 1901 and 1902, when he concentrated on this particular style, Mackintosh on the whole achieved great success, but he obviously realised that the style was an end in itself; while it released him from some restrictions, it imposed just as many new ones. When he next came to use the same motifs, he seems to have realised their limitations and began to evolve a more reasoned and mature style than that which found its ultimate expression in the Wärndorfer music salon.

Fritz Wärndorfer was a successful Viennese businessman and an enthusiastic patron of the group of architects, painters and designers who formed the Secession group. He had met Mackintosh in Glasgow in 1900, and they had seen each other again during the Mackintoshes' visit to Vienna, in about October or November 1900. There is no documentary evidence of any further meetings until April 1902, but at some point in the interim Wärndorfer commissioned a music salon from Mackintosh and, at the same time, a dining room from Josef Hoffmann. It was probably when he met Mackintosh in Turin in April 1902 that Wärndorfer bought the writing desk that was exhibited there, together with two gesso panels by Margaret and possibly also the cabinet that had previously been exhibited at the Secession in 1900. Wärndorfer wrote to Hoffmann on 29th April 1902, saying that Mackintosh had just sent him the full-size drawings for the furniture and wanted Wärndorfer to let him have any comments that Hoffmann might make on the designs. Wärndorfer goes on to say that Hoffmann's pupil, Max Schmidt, had looked over the structural drawings and that he was confused by Mackintosh's detailing of the projecting fireplace bay. Work probably started soon after June 1902, the date when the plans were presented to the authorities for the necessary permission to build. On 23rd December 1902, Wärndorfer again wrote to Hoffmann about both rooms and remarked that the music salon was almost finished, although he was still waiting for the piano.

Mackintosh's room was square, with two rectangular projections on adjacent walls, one for a fireplace ingle, the other for a large window bay

The Wärndorfer Music Salon, Vienna. *Above:* The only surviving photograph to show the piano and the window seat in the background. The piano, one of the largest pieces of furniture Mackintosh ever designed, is roughly square in plan, the sides decorated with high-relief carvings of stylised swooping birds. 1902.I. Piano, destroyed, 1902.16.

with fitted seating. The fireplace bay projected beyond the line of the original wall and internally it had a low ceiling the same height as the picture rail which encircled the rest of the room. The window similarly projected beyond the line of the salon wall and was enclosed by an arch in the shape of an inverted heart which linked the high backs of the fitted seats. The walls of the room were panelled to picture rail height, about two metres, with white-painted boards that had their butt joints hidden by a rounded cover strip. At the top of alternate strips were box-like features, which appear to have had an inlay of coloured glass and could have been be lampshades, although the room was well provided with light from four clusters of unshaded lamps hung with clear glass globes from an oval metal rail fixed to the ceiling. Above the picture rail on two opposite walls was a deep frieze (blank in surviving photographs, taken around 1903), for which the Mackintoshes designed two gesso panels on the theme of Maeterlinck's *The Seven Princesses*, which seem to have been executed in 1906. Photographs survive of two other panels by Margaret which were mounted on the piano; one of the reasons for the delay in finishing the piano was almost certainly their late arrival, as one is dated 1903.

The furniture in the room is all very similar to that designed for Kingsborough Gardens and the Turin Exhibition, and it was, of course, designed at almost the same time – in the first four months of 1902. The armchairs

A view looking towards the fireplace ingle, showing almost all the furniture except for the piano: the fireplace (wood, painted white, with panels of leaded glass) which is more in the proportion of one of Mackintosh's cabinets than his usual fireplaces; the fitted glazed cabinet (wood, painted white, with leaded glass doors); the table (wood, painted white, and inlaid with coloured glass) – unlike any other table designed by Mackintosh at this date, it has two broad splats carrying a carved motif, connecting the top and the lower shelf; the armchair with embroidered upholstered back (wood, painted white) – a repetition of the chair for Kingsborough Gardens, but here with the addition of embroidery (probably by Margaret Macdonald) on the back of each chair; chair with stencilled high back (wood, painted white, with upholstered seat and back), replicas of which were designed for the Turin Exhibition. 1902. J. All individual pieces destroyed. Fireplace, 1902.13. Fitted cabinet, 1902.15. Table, 1902.20. Armchair, 1902.21. Chair with stencilled back, 1902.22.

are the same as the Kingsborough Gardens chairs, but with the addition of embroidery on the back rests, while the tall white chairs are replicas of the one exhibited at Turin. Two tables in the room are new, but still very elegant in design: an oval table with ten legs is basically an elaboration of the one for Kingsborough Gardens, but the square table in the centre of the room is unlike any other that Mackintosh designed. It has simple square legs at each corner and a plain top and lower shelf connected by a broad vertical splat decorated with raised carving. The most impressive item in the room, however, was the piano, a massive piece about a metre high and two metres square. The upper part was solid and decorated with Mackintosh's favourite (but by this date uncommon) motif of a flying bird. The small gesso panels seem to have been over the keyboard; above them was a music stand of slender columns, each capped by a small cube. A contemporary witness, Ludwig Hevesi, described the salon as 'a place of spiritual joy' and 'an artistic curiosity of the first order'. It is sad, then, to relate that no trace of it – either furniture or panels – can be found. This is, without doubt, the most serious of the many acts of vandalism that Mackintosh's work seems to have suffered.

Above: Oval table for the Wärndorfer Music Salon, Vienna (wood, painted white, with inlaid decorative panels). Similar to the oval tea table made for Kingsborough Gardens but this has ten legs, grouped in fives at each end of the oval. The table illustrated is an identical example retained by Mackintosh and shown at Moscow in 1903. Art Institute of Chicago. 1902.19.

Below: *The Opera of the Wind* and *The Opera of the Sea.* These panels, about 30 cm. square, were inserted above the keyboard of the Wärndorfer Music Salon piano. 1902.G.

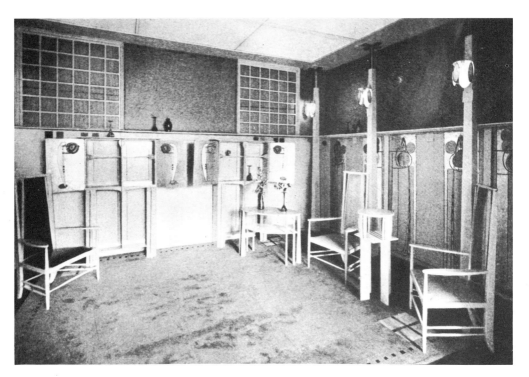

The Exhibition Room at Moscow. *Above:* Most of the furniture shown here had been designed for other commissions, but the carpet and the wall hangings were all new. 1903.A.

Below: A view into Mackintosh's room from that of another exhibitor. The chairs either side of the entrance arch are from the hall at Windyhill. 1903.B.

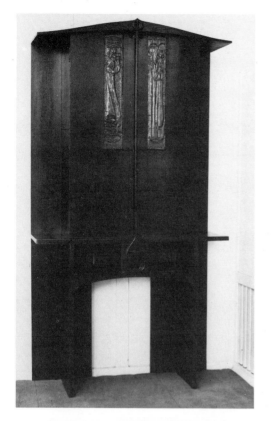

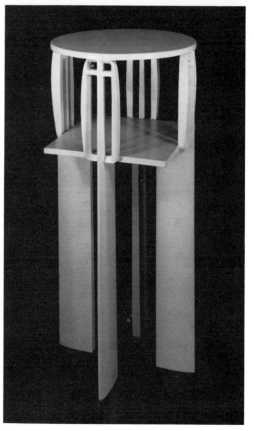

Top left: Smoker's cabinet (oak stained dark, with beaten copper panels by Margaret Macdonald). A replica for Mackintosh's own use of the cabinet that was made for him in 1899 but sold at the Vienna Secession exhibition to Hugo Henneberg for a house that was being designed for him by Josef Hoffmann. The original was in turn a more assured and successful development of the cabinet made for H. Brückmann in 1898. Glasgow School of Art. 1903.1.

Top right: Detail of smoker's cabinet. 1903.1.

Bottom left: Bookcase for Michael Diack (oak, stained dark, with glazed doors). 1903.2.

Bottom right: Small circular table with square projecting shelf (oak, painted white). The only new piece of furniture exhibited at Moscow. Hunterian Art Gallery, University of Glasgow. 1902.23.

Above: The Front Saloon, Willow Tea Rooms, Glasgow. This contemporary photograph shows the arrangement of the chairs and tables, the fitted seating, carpet and embroidered window curtains in the Front Saloon. T.& R. Annan, Glasgow. 1903.C.

THE WILLOW TEA ROOMS 1903

The most elegant of Miss Cranston's four Tea Rooms, the Willow Tea Rooms in Sauchiehall Street, opened in October 1904, but Mackintosh was at work designing it from the spring of 1903. Most of the furniture was designed from July to November 1903, but some pieces were still being added in 1905. It was the last complete suite of rooms that Mackintosh designed for Miss Cranston, although additions and alterations at Ingram Street were carried out piecemeal until about 1912, and Mackintosh returned to the Willow Tea Rooms in 1917 to add The Dug-Out in the basement.

The site chosen for the Tea Rooms was in Glasgow's most fashionable street. 'Sauchiehall' means 'alley of the willows', and the theme of young willows – both naturalistic and metaphorical – was used throughout the building. The Willow Tea Rooms were also notable as the only ones where Mackintosh was able to design the exteriors as well as the interiors. The site had frontage only to the north and south, as it was enclosed between existing buildings. The entrance was in the north elevation, which rose through four stories; on the south side, Mackintosh extended his building beyond the line of its neighbours, but this elevation was never intended for public view.

The variety and arrangement of the rooms was similar to those at the Argyle Street and Ingram Street Tea Rooms, with the addition of a special dining room, the first floor Room de Luxe, which was at the heart of the building and was unique in Mackintosh's *oeuvre*. The entrance was at ground level in Sauchiehall Street, and visitors were channelled to the foot of the main staircase past a long, white-painted panelled screen, with glass panels above, like that at Ingram Street. At the end of this corridor was the main cash desk, and here customers had the choice of entering the front or rear salooons or ascending the staircase to the gallery and the upper floors. The basement contained the cloakrooms and lavatories, and also the kitchens.

Willow Tea Rooms, Glasgow. *Opposite page. Left:* The Front Saloon. This photograph shows the screen (wood, painted white, and leaded glass) at the entrance. The umbrella stand (metal, painted black) is a simple design. 1903.D. Glass from screen, 1903.5. Umbrella stand, untraced, 1903.10. *Right:* The Front Saloon. The *baldacchino* (wood, stained dark, surmounted by a metal framework holding a glass vessel) is in the centre of the room. This strange structure was situated over a table for four in the centre of the Front Saloon. It consisted of five square posts, linked by spars, with four carved panels, one on each of the outer uprights. These took the form of stylised willow leaves and the whole composition was perhaps intended to symbolise a clump of willow trees. Behind the *baldacchino* is the staircase to the upper floors; beyond it one can see into the Back Saloon with the glazed screen of the Gallery above. 1903.E. *Baldacchino*, destroyed, 1903.6.

Willow Tea Rooms, Glasgow. *Top left:* Back Saloon looking south towards the fireplace. 1903.F. *Top right:* Wall-hangings in the Back Saloon. A detail showing the table settings and the stencilled canvas hangings. 1903.G. *Bottom left:* The Gallery, Willow Tea Rooms, Glasgow, looking down through the balustrade to the open well over the Back Saloon. The ceiling is supported on a series of tapering posts, some of which are themselves supported by beams across the light well. 1903.H. All Hunterian Art Gallery, University of Glasgow. *Bottom right:* The Gallery. A view of the south-east corner. T.& R. Annan, Glasgow. 1903.I.

The Front Saloon, the main room on the ground floor, was predominantly white. The panelled walls, screens, fireplace, ceiling and the plaster-relief frieze above the panelling were all painted white. In contrast, the movable furniture was dark-stained oak, but only the ladderback chairs were obvious, because the tables had white cloths which covered all but the bottom few inches of their legs, and the fitted seating, which was upholstered in velvet (probably purple or blue), was also hidden by the tables. In the centre of the room, positioned between the fireplace and the entrance, was a formal

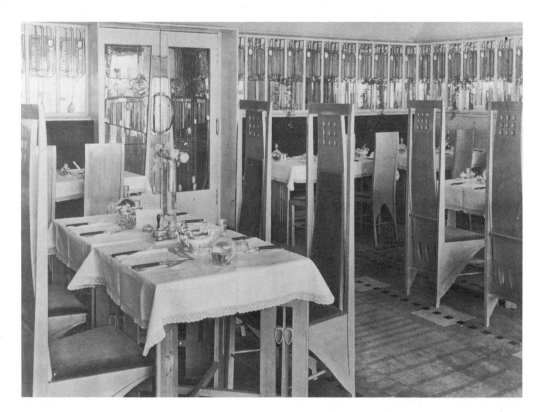

The Room de Luxe, Willow Tea Rooms, Glasgow. The square table (probably oak, painted silver, with coloured glass inserts) was designed to match the rest of the furniture in this room; most of the other tables used in the Tea Rooms were very simple. The tables and carpet have disappeared but examples of both types of chair survive. Hunterian Art Gallery, University of Glasgow. 1903.J. Table, 1903.25.

construction of dark-stained timber, which Thomas Howarth has described as a *baldacchino*. This supported a sculptural wrought iron cage which contained a large glass bowl, about one metre in diameter, in which were suspended glass tubes for holding long-stemmed flowers. Encircling this was a broad, flat band of black-painted iron, suspended by hoops from the ceiling, to which were attached unshaded electric lamps. This play between rounded and angular shapes was a theme that was repeated throughout the building.

The ceiling of the Front Saloon was almost 5.5 metres high, and Mackintosh introduced a series of low-relief panels in plaster as a frieze between it and the wall panelling. The design is based on willow trees, with their tendril-like branches and pointed leaves. Mackintosh turned it into a stylised pattern, the sources of which are obvious to the initiated, but which looks at first sight like a totally abstract sculpture nearly two metres high and just over nine metres long.

Projecting beyond the line of the upper stories was a hipped roof extension that housed two tea rooms, the Back Saloon and the Gallery. The Back Saloon opened directly on to the Front Saloon, but Mackintosh's handling of the two spaces indicated clearly that one was entering a different room. The ceiling was much lower than at the front, as the Gallery above could be seen from the Front Saloon through a glazed and wrought iron screen; the Gallery was almost a mezzanine floor, with a ceiling that was much lower than the first floor ceilings in the front of the building. The low ceiling – the floor of the gallery above – made the Back Saloon fairly dark, and the walls were divided by dark-stained wooden straps with grey panels between them to accentuate this. At intervals, the panels were decorated by stencilled canvas hangings, predominantly silver in colour. The fireplace at the back of the room was also stained dark, with a paler cement-rendered fire surround. It contained three elaborate mirror panels which reflected the light that filtered down from the gallery roof-lights through the open well in the centre of the room.

The furniture of the Back Saloon was also arranged to reflect the architecture: the semi-circular order desk chair sat at the junction of the Front and Back Saloons, its curve against the *baldacchino* in the white room. Down either side of the Back Saloon, the tables were at right angles to the walls, with six dark-stained ladderback chairs, arranged in two rows of three, at each table. In the centre of the room, in the gallery well and running between the fireplace and the order desk, the tables were placed at 45° to the walls with four armchairs at each table. Even the carpet emphasised this regularity: it was plain beneath the tables, but in the aisles it had a chequer-work pattern.

The main staircase, rising from the cash desk in the Front Saloon, had an open balustrade looking out over the tables beneath. The risers of the stair-

Billiards Room, Willow Tea Rooms, Glasgow. Mackintosh designed special billiards tables for all the Cranston Tea Rooms except Buchanan Street. Hunterian Art Gallery, University of Glasgow, 1903.M. Billiards table, untraced, 1903.35.

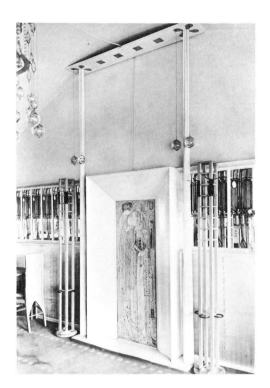

Right: Crystal chandelier, Room de Luxe, Willow Tea Rooms, Glasgow – the most elaborate chandelier designed by Mackintosh. Hidden among the glass balls was a group of electric lamps attached either to the upper circular rail or pendant. Sadly it has not survived. Hunterian Art Gallery, University of Glasgow. 1903.L.

Left: Gesso panel, Willow Tea Rooms, Glasgow. The gesso panel, illustrating D.G. Rossetti's sonnet 'O ye, all ye that walk in Willowwood' was made by Margaret Macdonald. T.& R. Annan, Glasgow. 1903.K.

case were stencilled with black and white checks in a pyramidal shape. The balustrade was formed of steel rods, about two centimetres in diameter, one rising from each tread, terminating in a rail at ceiling height. Between each rod, at the top, was fixed a panel of wrought iron, bent into an abstract pattern, from which hung green glass balls on stout wires.

From the first landing, one entered the Gallery Tea Room, which had tables grouped round three sides of the well, with views down into the Back Saloon. On the fourth side, the north, was a corridor with a glazed and wrought iron screen at low level, looking out over the Front Saloon. The ceiling was made up of exposed beams, creating an egg-box effect, and was supported by eight tapering columns, which were circular at their bases but became square about 60 cm. from the top. The columns were arranged in two rows of four, dividing the room into three parts; the four central columns sprang from the two heavy beams that crossed the light well. The ceiling above this well was solid, but the two side-aisles had open ceilings which admitted light from the glazed panels in the roof. The woodwork, including the ceiling, was all painted white, as was the fireplace in the south wall. The furniture, of the same pattern as in the ground floor saloons, was stained dark. The walls were also dark, with strips of white paint creating an effect of panelling, around which was stencilled a black trellis pattern surmounted by two stylised roses.

Above: Cash desk for the Willow Tea Rooms, Glasgow (wood, painted white). The desk was situated at the foot of the staircase at the end of the screen by the entrance so that all the patrons of the Tea Room were forced to pass it. More elaborate than the desk at the Ingram Street Tea Rooms, it is decorated with a series of carved shapes like the eyes in peacock feathers. Destroyed. 1903.4.

Top right: Smoking Room, Willow Tea Rooms, Glasgow. The table (ebonised wood) is one of the earliest designs that emphasise the square as a decorative motif. 1903.N. Table, untraced, 1903.39.

Bottom right: Ladderback chair for the Willow Tea Rooms, Glasgow (ebonised oak). Mackintosh's succinct rationalisation of the traditional ladderback design. Over 130 of these chairs were made. Glasgow School of Art. 1903.8.

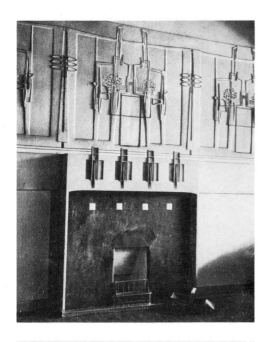

Willow Tea Rooms, Glasgow. *Top left:*
Fireplace for the Front Saloon (wood, painted
white). The four carved motifs in the top of the
fireplace reappear in the Smoking Room and
the Ladies' Rest Room. This fireplace was
destroyed by Mackintosh in 1917 when he
placed the entrance to The Dug-Out Tea Room
here. Destroyed. 1903.11.

Top right: Stool (ebonised oak). An extremely
compact design relying for inspiration entirely
on geometrical motifs. Glasgow School of Art.
1903.13.

Bottom left: Armchair (oak, stained
dark or ebonised). A sturdy but not particularly
comfortable chair. A very boxy design,
consisting basically of three flat squares of
timber forming two sides and a back. 1903.14.

Bottom right: Fireplace for the Back Saloon
(wood, stained dark, with inlaid panels). Like
all the fireplaces at the Willow this is very
simple. The grate is a commercial design and is
surrounded by a plain cement render inset with
tiles and glass panels. *In situ.* 1903.17.

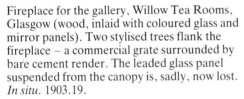

Fireplace for the gallery, Willow Tea Rooms, Glasgow (wood, inlaid with coloured glass and mirror panels). Two stylised trees flank the fireplace – a commercial grate surrounded by bare cement render. The leaded glass panel suspended from the canopy is, sadly, now lost. *In situ.* 1903.19.

Circular table with five legs for the Room de Luxe, Willow Tea Rooms, Glasgow (pine, originally painted silver). The carved decoration is identical with that on the square table and this piece was probably positioned in the centre of the room at the bow window. Glasgow School of Art. 1903.26.

On the first floor, overlooking Sauchiehall Street, was the most important of the rooms, the Room de Luxe or Ladies' Room. It is one of the most precious interiors that Mackintosh ever designed, and if Margaret had a hand in any of his designs, it was surely in this. The north wall was made wholly of a window, with panels of mirror-glass in the leaded panes. Leaded mirror-glass panels formed a frieze above stretched silk panelling on the other three walls, each wall being broken at its centre by doors, a fireplace, or a gesso panel. Fitted seating against the walls was upholstered in purple, and the loose chairs were painted silver, those at the centre tables having high backs with nine insets of leaded glass. The double doors contained leaded glass panels, the most elaborate that Mackintosh ever designed, but the gesso panel was by Margaret and was based on Dante Gabriel Rossetti's sonnet, 'O ye, all ye that walk in Willowwood'. The ceiling was barrel-vaulted; in the centre hung a crystal chandelier with balls, ovals and tear-drops of solid glass that reflected the light from the electric lamps in their midst. Here ladies gathered for coffee, luncheon and afternoon tea in a haven of silver and purple dominated by the melancholy gesso panel and the glittering chandelier.

Certainly Margaret's influence is to be seen in the theme of the room, with its associations with the Pre-Raphaelite concepts of love and anguish, but in the handling of the spaces and the design of the furniture there is a move away from the limitations of such a dream world. The wall decorations may still use organic motifs, but here they are set in leaded glass and are far less frivolous in their linear patterns than the stencils at Kingsborough Gardens.

As with all the other furniture designed for the Willow Tea Rooms, organic motifs are banished from the decoration of the chairs and tables in the Room de Luxe, with the exception of stylised leaves inset in the legs of

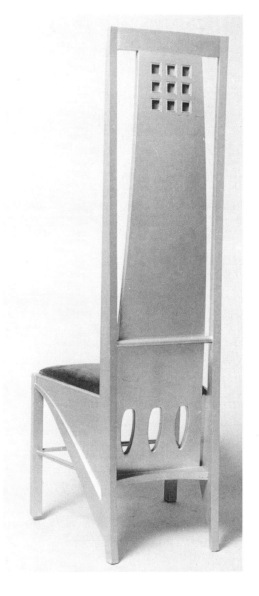

Willow Tea Rooms, Glasgow. *Above:* Chair for the Room de Luxe (oak painted silver, upholstered in velvet). Hunterian Art Gallery, University of Glasgow; National Museum of Antiquities of Scotland, Edinburgh; Victoria and Albert Museum, London. 1903.23.

Right: Chair with high back for the Room de Luxe (oak, painted silver, with coloured glass inserts and upholstered in purple velvet). One of the most famous of Mackintosh's chairs, this and other pieces for the Room de Luxe are the only items to have been painted silver. Hunterian Art Gallery, University of Glasgow; Graves Art Gallery, Sheffield. 1903.20.

the tables. The emphasis is on ovals and squares, but the heaviness of the Argyle Street – and even some of the Ingram Street – furniture has also gone. The elegance of the 1902 designs remains, but it is by no means as emphatic or mannered. All these new designs are rather understated, more subtle and quieter than anything produced for Turin or the Wärndorfer Salon. At the Willow Tea Rooms, white walls and table-cloths contrast with dark-stained or ebonised chairs; in the Room de Luxe, purple silk, purple and white glass, and silvered mirrors reflect the choice of purple and silver for the chairs and tables. The all-white rooms of 1902 have given way to a deliberate contrast of an architectural rather than pictorial composition. This does not mean, though, that Mackintosh totally rejected the achievements of 1902. Some furniture is still painted and stretches the limits of traditional methods of construction; roses still appear in leaded glass and stencilled hangings; balls of glass hang over the staircases, and crystal balls

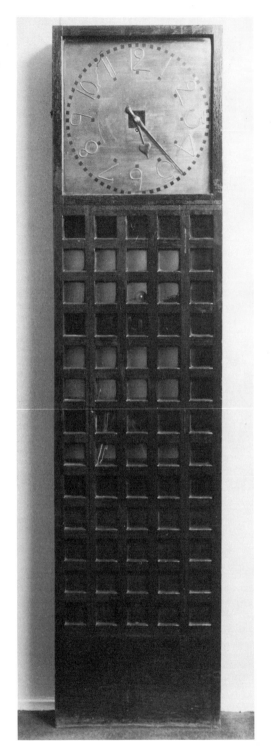

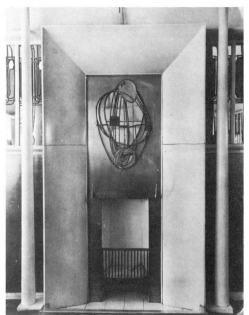

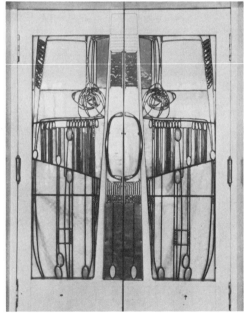

Willow Tea Rooms, Glasgow. *Left:* Clock (oak, stained dark, with polished steel face and brass numerals, and glazed door). One of the most rigorously geometrical pieces designed for the Willow, making extensive use of the square in its decoration. Glasgow School of Art. 1903.31.

Top right: Mackintosh frequently used a design like a giant picture frame for some of the simpler of these Tea Room fireplaces. This one neatly encloses a plain metal fire surround on which hung a fine piece of leaded glass (now lost). *In situ.* 1903.29.

Bottom right: Doors for the Room de Luxe (pine, painted white, with metal handles and leaded glass). Mackintosh's most elaborate and certainly his largest design in leaded glass. The theme is again the willow, with stylised leaves and waving stems, combined with his favourite motif of an opening rose. *In situ.* 1903.30.

Willow Tea Rooms. *Top left:* Fitted seating for the Billiards Room (pine, stained dark, with rush seats and leather backs). Untraced. 1903.36.

Top right: Table for the Billiards Room (ebonised oak). A robust, even crude, design for the masculine preserve of the Billiards Room. Glasgow School of Art. 1903.37.

Bottom left: Fireplace for the Billiards Room (ebonised pine, with wrought iron grate and tiled fire-surround). A very simple timber structure enhanced by an elaborate wrought iron grate flanked by tall candle holders. Victoria and Albert Museum, London. 1903.38.

Bottom right: Square table (ebonised wood with coloured glass inlay). Possibly designed for the Willow Tea Rooms, Glasgow about 1903. Glasgow School of Art. 1903.41a.

decorate the Room de Luxe. Yet these elements are kept in their place and not allowed to take over the interiors; they complement the furniture and do not overpower it.

The second floor of the Willow Tea Rooms probably contained the Billiards Room and the Smoking Room, although subsequent alterations have obscured the layout of this floor. There is yet another room at the Willow Tea Rooms that cannot be explained satisfactorily: at second-floor level in the adjacent property to the east was a room panelled in a typical Mackintosh style. It also had a fireplace almost identical with the Billiards Room fireplace (which is now in the Victoria & Albert Museum), although its tiles are patterned rather than plain. It seems possible that this room was added either around 1905, when Mackintosh was designing more furniture for the Willow Tea Rooms, or around 1917, when he designed The Dug-Out in the basement of the building to the west. Possibly it was created later still by the Kensington Restaurant (which acquired the premises in the 1920s) out of panelling and glass removed from other rooms, particularly those on the second floor. This would explain the patterned tiles in the fireplace; if it is actually the fireplace from the Smoking Room (which was illustrated in *Dekorative Kunst* and was almost identical to that in the Billiards Room), the tiles would probably have had to be renewed when it was moved. It is not impossible that the Kensington created the fittings to harmonise with the existing Mackintosh features, as they took good care of the designs, unlike their successors, Daly's department store.

When Daly's was sold in 1978, the developers made some attempt at recreating the interiors of the Willow Tea Rooms (a condition, in fact, of planning permission), including the reinstatement of the original ground floor elevation, which had been destroyed by Daly's. The final plans approved by the local authority and the developers allowed for extensive restoration or reproduction of the original fittings. Most of this work was

concentrated on the ground floor and involved replacement of the plaster panels at frieze level, a reproduction of the Front Saloon fireplace, re-modelling of the Gallery ceiling and replacement of the beams and columns in the well, and reproduction of the stencil decoration around the Gallery. The restoration of 1979-80 has helped recapture some of the original appearance and atmosphere of the Tea Rooms. The Willow is again a self-contained building, as the east wall of the Front Saloon, which was removed by Daly's, has been reinstated. Replicas of the plaster frieze panels have been installed along the east and west walls of the Front Saloon, and a reconstruction has been made of the original entrance and window, although the small leaded glass panes have been omitted. The fireplaces of the Back Saloon and Gallery have been uncovered and the rear windows reinstated. Perhaps the most effective part of the restoration, however, is the rebuilding of the false ceiling above the Gallery, and the replacement of the beams across the light well and the tapering columns that rise from them to support the ceiling.

Windyhill, Kilmacolm. *Left:* Trellis work arbour (red pine, painted white). A rigidly geometrical design, located in the north-west corner of the garden. It was originally surmounted by a wrought-iron finial. *In situ.* 1903.44.

Right: Dovecote (yellow pine). Mackintosh was happy to design even this smallest of 'houses' for a client and friend like William Davidson. Destroyed. 1903.45.

Opposite page: Semi-circular garden seat (probably red pine). Situated at the foot of this steep hill-side garden, it was oriented to get the best of the sun although Mackintosh had originally (1901) intended to site it in the northern part of the garden, facing the house. Destroyed. 1903.42.

Window seat in the drawing room, The Hill House, Helensburgh. Royal Commission on the Ancient and Historical Monuments of Scotland. 1903.73.

Fireplace in the drawing room, The Hill House, Helensburgh. A contemporary photograph taken before the removal of the ceiling light-fittings; it also shows one of Mr Blackie's more conventional chairs which were used alongside the furniture which Mackintosh designed for the house. Royal Commission on the Ancient and Historical Monuments of Scotland. 1903.R.

The main bedroom, The Hill House, Helensburgh, looking east. As furnished in 1903, with the two rugs and the wall stencilling in place. Royal Commission on the Ancient and Historical Monuments of Scotland. 1903.S.

THE HILL HOUSE, 1903-04

Mackintosh's most important domestic commission was The Hill House at Helensburgh, built for the Glasgow publisher, Walter W. Blackie, on a hilltop with superb views of the Firth of Clyde. The planning and decoration of the interiors, as of the exteriors, were a refinement of the themes used at Windyhill and for the *Haus eines Kunstfreundes* – on a larger scale than the former, but by no means as elaborate or expansive as the German competition designs.

Blackie wanted a family house, a practical and efficient place to live. Mackintosh gave him all he wanted, paying obsessive attention to the details that transformed it from an efficient machine into a living work of art. The plan is similar to that for the *Haus eines Kunstfreundes*, but differing particularly in the axial entrance on the west façade. Like the competition designs, The Hill House segregates the men from the women and children. Blackie wanted a library, which he also used as a study and business room; this is situated just off the first hallway and, in the original plans, a billiards room and cloakroom balanced it on the opposite side of this small hall. In this way, Blackie could meet and entertain his business callers without upsetting the domestic routine of the drawing room.

Moving east along this entrance axis, visitors for the family would advance out of the small, dark hall up four steps into the main hall, a bright room with light coming from the staircase windows and from its own windows, which look out on the north courtyard. It is furnished as a reception room with chairs and a table, and a splendid fireplace and panelled walls as at Windyhill. The wall between the panelling is stencilled with an abstract pattern based on geometrical and organic motifs. The main axis from the front door effectively ends in this hall, where doors lead off to the drawing room and the dining room, as its continuation is only into the service quarters. All the main rooms are placed at 90° to the axis of the hall, and even starting to climb the staircase involves a 180° turn. After only four steps, one encounters a small ingle with a fitted seat overlooking the hall fireplace through a lath screen. To ascend further means turning through another 90° to a half landing, apsidal as at Windyhill, and turning again through 180° to the first floor landing where the east-west axis returns along the bedroom corridor.

Although the drawing room has a much smaller area than he provided for the *Haus eines Kunstfreundes*, Mackintosh devised a plan that gives it various quite separate functions. Directly opposite the door from the hall is a wide window seat, flanked by fitted book and magazine racks. This seat is contained in a bay with a lower ceiling than the rest of the room and is expressed outside as a stark, glazed projection from the main elevation of the house. The bay has a wide view over Helensburgh and the Clyde; it was

The Hill House, Helensburgh. *Left:* The hall. A contemporary photograph looking west towards the main door and showing the foot of the staircase. Royal Commission on the Ancient and Historical Monuments of Scotland. 1903.P.

Right: The library. The chairs seen in this photograph were brought into the library from the hall. Hunterian Art Gallery, University of Glasgow. 1903.O.

Opposite page. The main bedroom, looking west. A modern photograph, taken after the removal of the wall stencilling. The concave recesses that form the bedside cupboards (oak, painted white, with leaded glass panels) became a favourite motif and were repeated at Hous'hill and in the Chinese and Cloister Rooms at the Ingram Street Tea Rooms, Glasgow, in 1911-12. The bed (oak, painted white) has no headboard as the top of the bed was designed to fit into a deep niche formed by the two bedside cupboards. The foot of the bed is decorated with a high-relief carving, rather like the bed at Windyhill, Kilmacolm. 1903.T. Bedside cupboards, *in situ* (National Trust for Scotland), 1903.53. Bed, *in situ* (National Trust for Scotland), 1903.54.

effectively a summer room, with central heating under the seat to provide some warmth when the weather was cold. In winter, domestic life was concentrated around the fireplace on the wall opposite the bay window. With only a much smaller window to let in winter light from the south, this part of the room was warmer, and the furniture, particularly the large couch, was so arranged as to shut out the colder bay and the draughts from the hall. At the far end of the room was another bay, formed by reducing the height of the ceiling, in which was kept the grand piano. This large piece of furniture had its own carefully defined territory so that it did not encroach, spatially at least, on the rest of the drawing room.

The floors of the two bays were bare boards, but the main part of the drawing room, defined by the full-height ceiling, was carpeted. The design, like that of the hall carpet, was of squares laid out in a perimeter aisle. In 1904, the lighting of the room was provided by four large glass and metal fittings, each combining the motifs of the circle and the square. There was no cornice between wall and ceiling, both of which were originally painted white; below the moulding that encircled the room at door and fireplace level the walls were stencilled with a pattern of roses in green and pink contained in a framework of stencilled silver panels with chequered decoration.

In November 1905, quotations were obtained for wall lights to replace the four ceiling fittings; these were paid for in February 1906. Some of the furniture for the room was also made in 1905, including the clock, the lampshade and the easy chair. In 1912, Mackintosh visited The Hill House to advise on redecoration and the repair and recovering of some of the pieces. Mackintosh's notes at the time quite clearly state that the drawing room ceiling was to be painted 'plum'. The most likely reason for this new colour scheme was to redress the balance between the ceiling and the rest of the room after it was disturbed by the removal of the four large light fittings. These had been fixed to the ceiling, and their lower edges were level with the tops of the doors and the fireplace. They provided a continuation of this specific level, about 2.4 metres above the floor, especially when they were alight: as the gas jets were in the lower part of the fitting, they would have distracted attention from the ceiling. When they were replaced by wall lamps, the ceiling was left bare, and this large, unbroken plane became much more dominant in the composition of the room than had been intended. By darkening it, Mackintosh attempted to reduce the reflectiveness of the ceiling and thus its impact on the rest of the room. At present (1984), however, the ceiling is painted black because of a mistaken identification of the colour under the dirt at a point when it had not been repainted for over 50 years. The suggestion behind this step was that Mackintosh had painted the ceiling black because of the dirty marks that were continually made by the gas wall lamps, although these can have been no worse than similar marks in rooms elsewhere in the house where ceilings were not painted a dark colour.

In recent years, the house has been undergoing extensive repair and restoration, and the drawing room wall stencils, which were over-painted in the 1950s, have been replaced. The ceiling, however, remains black and

The Hill House, Helensburgh.
Left: Fitted wardrobes in the main bedroom (pine, painted white, with coloured glass inserts). Mackintosh made two ranges of wardrobes, along the east and north walls of the room. Those on the east wall are set into a bay, which runs the length of the wall, as does the couch. Their carved decoration is firmly based on organic motifs. *In situ* (National Trust for Scotland). 1903.51.
Right: Chair for the main bedroom (ebonised oak). A stark contrast to the white paint of the woodwork and all the other furniture in the room (except the stool). These two chairs are delicate and spidery and were used to articulate the two separate areas of the room, the sleeping area and the sitting room adjacent to the fire. Moving either of the chairs from the position which Mackintosh allocated to these destroys the subtle balance of the room. *In situ* (National Trust for Scotland). 1903.58.

has the opposite effect to that which Mackintosh intended, as it is now so harsh and so obviously out of balance that one is immediately aware of it, and it again overpowers the room.

The dining room, like all of Mackintosh's earlier domestic dining rooms, has dark walls, a pale ceiling and concentrated pools of light over the table and around the fireplace. The walls are panelled here with pine, which was originally stained dark, but has been bleached almost to its natural colour;

Mackintosh's earliest decorative motifs with the new geometric shapes which were to become dominant in his work. *In situ* (National Trust for Scotland). 1903.52.

Bottom left: Square table for the main bedroom (oak, painted white). *In situ* (National Trust for Scotland). 1903.55.

Right: Cheval mirror for the main bedroom (oak, painted white, with coloured glass inlay). A development of the mirror made for Windyhill, Kilmacolm, the main differences being the more elaborate top, the larger trays and wider pedestals supporting them, and the pierced grid of nine squares in each pedestal. This grid echoes the leaded glass pattern in the wardrobes on the north wall. *In situ* (National Trust for Scotland). 1903.57.

The Hill House, Helensburgh. *Top left:* Washstand for the main bedroom (wood, painted white, with a silver-painted top and a leaded glass upstand). A simple wooden structure with an elaborately patterned upstand, this piece combines some of

the ceiling and the upper parts of the walls are painted white. A simple fireplace on the south wall is flanked by two elaborate wall lights (which are duplicated on the north wall). A single light fitting was suspended over the dining table; this now hangs on the staircase ingle.

In the service quarters, the store, pantry, larder and kitchen all have fitted cupboards of a simple design, but unmistakably Mackintosh's own.

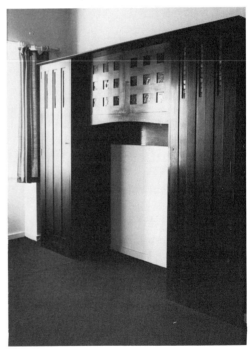

The Hill House, Helensburgh. *Top left:* Dressing table for the main bedroom (oak, painted white). *In situ* (National Trust for Scotland). 1903.59. *Top right:* Fireplace for the main bedroom (wood, painted white, the grate surrounded by sheet steel inset with coloured glass panels). The fire-surround is one of Mackintosh's most original. It appears, in turn, both severe and luxurious – the bright, shiny metal coldly reflecting the whiteness of the woodwork and then the glow of the hot coals. *In situ* (National Trust for Scotland). 1903.60.

Bottom left: Chest of drawers and mirror for the dressing room (mahogany, French-polished, with inserts of coloured glass). *In situ* (National Trust for Scotland). 1903.63. *Bottom right:* Wardrobe for the dressing room (mahogany, French-polished, with inserts of coloured glass). Designed to fit around an existing chest of drawers (not designed by Mackintosh) and to match it in colour and finish. *In situ* (National Trust for Scotland). 1903.64.

Similar cupboards were designed for The Moss at Dumgoyne, Stirlingshire, in 1907. At The Hill House, the first floor corridor, like that at Windyhill, contains linen cupboards and a fitted alcove seat looking out to the north. The corridor repeats the east-west axis of the entrance hall, with the bedrooms similarly ranged off it to the south. Most of the rooms have no fittings other than very simple fireplaces, with small panels of stencil decoration on the walls. Apart from the main bedroom, the only rooms of interest upstairs are the day nursery on the first floor and the playroom on the second floor. In the day nursery, which faces east, a full-height bow window echoes that of the breakfast room in the *Haus eines Kunstfreundes* which is similarly positioned. The playroom also refers to the competition design with its polygonal bay window looking out over the service wing and the garden.

A further similarity to the *Haus eines Kunstfreundes* design is the positioning of the main bedroom at the end of the corridor, out of the way of all the other bedrooms and well away from the children's rooms. A dressing room for Mr Blackie is attached. Mackintosh has attempted to define the different functions the main bedroom had to fulfil. As one enters, the

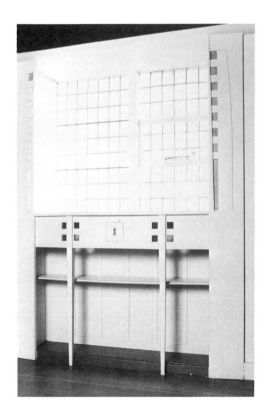

The Hill House, Helensburgh. *Left:* Window table in the drawing room (pine, painted white, with inserts of coloured glass). This table was fitted into the reveals of the window opposite the fireplace; the dominant motif is again the square. *In situ* (National Trust for Scotland). 1903.69. *Right:* Inglenook on the first-floor landing (pine, stained dark). A repetition of a similar feature used at Windyhill, again with a view to the north. *In situ* (National Trust for Scotland). 1903.67.

The Hill House, Helensburgh. *Left:* Fireplace for the drawing room (pine, painted white, with a gesso panel by Margaret Macdonald Mackintosh; steel grate with polished steel firedogs and fender, and mosaic surround with glass inlay). A design which successfully combines individual motifs found in other fireplaces at Windyhill, 120 Mains Street and the Willow Tea Rooms. The semi-circular niche of the fireplace cabinet (pine, painted white, with leaded glass panel) echoes the bedside cupboards but is here combined with a stylised 'tree' formed by the decoration of the shelves beneath. *In situ* (National Trust for Scotland). 1903.71. Fireplace cabinet, *in situ* (National Trust for Scotland), 1903.72. *Right:* Fireplace for the library (pine, dark stained, with coloured glass inserts). A business room and a study for Mr Blackie, which is simpler and more restrained than any room at The Hill House other than the dining room. Mackintosh incorporated cupboards and racks and even a small drop-down writing desk in the fittings either side of the fireplace. *In situ* (National Trust for Scotland). 1903.74.

room appears rectangular, with a flat ceiling; to the left is the fireplace, with at right angles to it a wall of fitted furniture – a settle and wardrobes. In fact, the room is L-shaped, and the large area to the west is occupied by the bed and more fitted wardrobes. This sleeping alcove is defined by a vaulted ceiling, the curve of the vault echoed by a curved bay on its south wall through which a small window admits daylight to the bed. In his original drawing, Mackintosh showed a screen of glass and timber with curtains at the junction of the vault with the flat ceiling. This would effectively have partitioned the bed from the more public part of the room, with its fireplace and couch; it was, however, not executed.

Mackintosh was designing movable furniture for The Hill House from November 1903, starting with the main bedroom, until the autumn of 1904, some months after the Blackies moved in. From the start, Walter Blackie made it clear that he could not afford to furnish his house entirely with new pieces. Mackintosh therefore concentrated on designing specific areas *in toto*, rather than diluting the overall effect by providing some new pieces for every room in the house. Only in the main bedroom and the hall was all the furniture made to Mackintosh's designs. The dining room had no movable furniture by Mackintosh and nor did Blackie's library, which was fully fitted by Mackintosh with shelving, cupboards and fireplace; for photographs of the library published in *Dekorative Kunst* in 1905 and probably taken in the summer of 1904, the hall chairs were moved into the library to give the appearance of a unified overall design. Blackie probably extended his commission to include pieces of furniture not originally requested, like

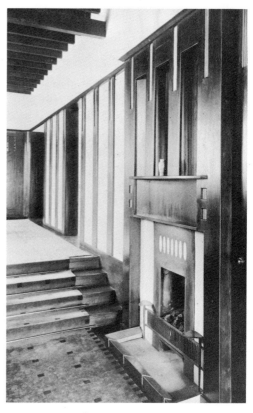

The Hill House, Helensburgh. *Left:* Fireplace for the dining room (pine, stained dark, with polished steel fire-surround and inlaid coloured glass and tiles). *In situ* (National Trust for Scotland). 1903.76. *Right:* Fireplace for the hall (pine, stained dark, with coloured and leaded glass inserts). A spatially complicated design, composed around the play between solid and void, and curved and flat planes. Seen to its best advantage from the seat in the staircase landing. *In situ* (National Trust for Scotland). 1903.77.

the writing desk and cabinet, which were designed in October and November 1904 and probably not delivered until the spring of 1905. Even then, Blackie did not consider the house to be completely furnished, and Mackintosh was still providing furniture for the drawing room as late as 1908. In 1912, when the interiors seemed absolutely finished, he turned to the garden and designed a bench for the terrace.

It is possible to attribute some of the developments in Mackintosh's style at the Willow Tea Rooms to the need for the furniture to be stronger than the domestic furniture designed in 1902; as the style adopted at Kingsborough Gardens could not easily have been combined with strength, Mackintosh would have been forced to look for a more rugged mode of expression. Strength, however, was no more important an element of the designs for The Hill House than it had been at Kingsborough Gardens, but still Mackintosh chose to move away from the rather feminine style. There are still stencil decorations on the walls, but the rose motif is combined with lattice in the bedroom, and in the drawing room it is contained within a more obviously architectural framework. The stencils in the hall are the work of the adventurous Mackintosh rather than the predictable Margaret Macdonald and are another abstract composition like the panels at the Willow Tea Rooms.

The only room at The Hill House to have movable white furniture is the bedroom; in the drawing room only the fitted furniture, such as the window seat and the fireplace, was painted white. One might have expected the bedroom to be an ideal situation in which Mackintosh could continue the style of the Rose Boudoir, but again the final design is tempered by a greater restraint and simplicity of decoration. There is a stronger emphasis on straight, clean lines, and such carved decoration as is used on the furniture is less literal in its imagery than that on, say, the Wärndorfer chairs or the Kingsborough Gardens cabinets. There is again a contrast between black furniture, for example the chairs and stool, and white fittings such as the fireplace and the wardrobes. The chairs are perhaps the most delicate items that Mackintosh ever designed, but their elegant appearance is not achieved with any of the stylistic devices of 1902. The grain is exposed, the stretchers and legs are as thin as, if not thinner than those of the Turin chairs and they are as attenuated as the Wärndorfer chairs. The design is simply stated, the fragility of the construction is accepted, not hidden by enamel, and no new structural techniques are used or even implied by the appearance of the chair. Above all, there is no trace of any organic decoration. From the careful use of a traditional ladderback and its combination with a pattern of pierced squares, Mackintosh produced a radically new stylistic vocabulary. One could say that this bedroom was transitional: the screen with figurative panels proposed in some of the drawings was not used, and squares appear alongside naturalistic motifs in some items such as the mirror and wardrobes.

Bedroom at the Dresdener Werkstatten für Handwerkskunst, which replicates several features from the main bedroom at The Hill House. 1903.V.

Most important of all, the furniture relates to the architectural spaces of the room; it does not overpower it or try to disguise the shape of the apartment, as at Kingsborough Gardens.

In exhibition work that is more or less contemporary with the Helensburgh bedroom, Mackintosh was prepared to go even further, as in the design for a bedroom for the Dresdener Werkstätten für Handwerkskunst in 1903-04. The inspiration for the design, particularly the layout of the furniture and the architectural features, is the white bedroom at The Hill House. There is, however, a much more definite commitment to the new geometrical style, to the extent of the almost total exclusion of organic decoration – the square is the dominant decorative motif. This more rigorous decoration makes the designs appear even more severely elegant than those for The Hill House, but the wall colour, a pale grey with stencilled squares of a darker shade, would have removed the dazzling effect of white furniture against white walls. There was a bow window, much larger in scale than that at The Hill House, and the ceiling, at least over the bed head, was shown in the drawing as vaulted. Behind each bed hung an embroidered panel which introduced the only note of organic decoration in the room: it was patterned with roses between a network of squares and straps, rather like the stencilling at The Hill House. Other features reminiscent of the Blackies' bedroom are the concave glass-panelled recesses in the bedside cupboards, the decoration of the splash-back of the washstand and the carved decoration at the foot of the beds.

The items contained in the room, none of which has survived, are again similar to those designed for The Hill House: two single beds, two fitted bedside cupboards, sofa, linen cupboard, cheval mirror, dressing table, fitted wardrobe, fireplace, medicine cupboard, washstand and three high-backed chairs and an armchair for the dressing table. All of this furniture may well have been purchased in Dresden, as it does not seem to have been returned to Glasgow, the usual fate of unsold items from other European exhibitions.

The Dresden designs raise the question of whether the replacement of the cursive elegance of the Rose Boudoir by a linear precision of a more Germanic or Austrian nature was deliberately done to appeal to possible clients in Dresden or if Mackintosh truly wished to forsake the natural forms that he had used so beautifully in earlier work. At Hous'hill, his next major domestic commission, there was again a mixture of organic and geometrical styles, but there can be little doubt that by then it was the geometrical that intrigued Mackintosh.

During the spring and summer of 1904, Mackintosh was working on the rest of the pieces for The Hill House and the furnishing of Hous'hill. At the same time, he was presumably also supervising the installation of the fittings at the Willow Tea Rooms. The furniture designed for Walter Blackie in 1904 repeats the rather transitional state reached in his bedroom, which had been designed late in 1903. Some pieces relate to the more linear style of the bedroom chairs for The Hill House. At Hous'hill there are similar disparities: the drawing and music room is more consciously feminine, but the hall and bedroom furniture is predominantly rectilinear and sets the

The Hill House, Helensburgh. *Top left:* Umbrella stand for the cloakroom (ebonised pine). *In situ* (National Trust for Scotland). 1904.2.

Top right: Towel rail for the cloakroom (ebonised pine). *In situ* (National Trust for Scotland). 1904.5.

Bottom left: Hat, coat and shoe rack for the cloakroom, (ebonised pine). *In situ* (National Trust for Scotland). 1904.3.

Bottom right: Hall chair (oak, varnished, with rush seat). One of Mackintosh's most satisfying designs for a chair. The hall at The Hill House was more than just a simple reception area, and all the furniture designed for it has a strong visual impact. *In situ* (National Trust for Scotland). 1904.6.

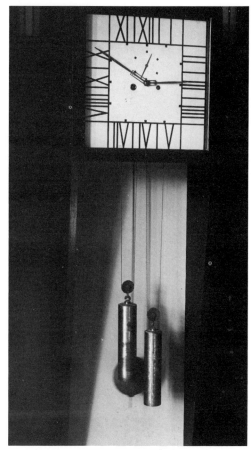

The Hill House, Helensburgh. *Top left:* Hall table (oak, varnished). The square cut-outs in the legs match those in the chairs, and the legs are placed at right-angles to each other, and do not follow the line of the top as do the earlier oval tables. *In situ* (National Trust for Scotland). 1904.7.

Centre left: Armchair for the drawing room (oak, lacquered black). A variant of the white chair designed for Kingsborough Gardens in 1902. *In situ* (National Trust for Scotland). 1904.10.

Bottom left: Couch for the drawing room, The Hill House, Helensburgh (mahogany, stained dark, with upholstered seat and back). Turned to face the fire, this chair effectively screened the user from the winter draughts of the winds off the Clyde. *In situ* (National Trust for Scotland). 1904.11.

Right: Hall clock (pine, stained dark, with painted metal face). *In situ* (National Trust for Scotland). 1904.8.

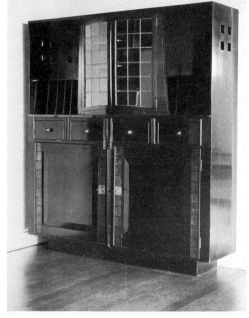

The Hill House, Helensburgh. *Opposite page. Above:* Writing desk (ebonised wood, with inlays of mother-of-pearl, metal and glass). One of the finest of Mackintosh's designs, produced after much discussion with Mr Blackie and the rejection of two other designs. That Mackintosh was well pleased with it is witnessed by his making another example for his own use. This latter desk, now in the Hunterian Art Gallery, varies slightly in having a taller central section for the storage of drawings etc., and the substitution of fruitwood inlay for the mother-of-pearl on the doors. 1904.13. *Top left:* Candlesticks (ebonised wood, with mother-of-pearl inlay and silver cups). These candlesticks make an assymetrical pair, one with mother-of-pearl inlay and the other without. Mackintosh also made an indentical pair for his own use. Glasgow Art Gallery; British Museum, London. 1904.18. *Bottom left:* Oval tea table for the drawing room (ebonised wood), Museum of Modern Art, New York. 1904.19A. *Right:* Chair (sycamore, lacquered black), designed to accompany the desk for Mr Blackie. Mackintosh later repeated the design for his own use. The design recalls the lattice pattern of the Order Desk chair at the Willow Tea Rooms (1904). Glasgow Art Gallery. 1904.17. *This page. Left:* Dressing table stool for the main bedroom (ebonised wood, with upholstered seat). The colour of the stool matches the two ladderback chairs designed in 1903. *In situ* (National Trust for Scotland). 1904.19. *Right:* Cabinet for the drawing room (ebonised pine, with glazed upper doors, inlaid with mother-of-pearl and stained sycamore). A large and complex design, borrowing some features from rejected designs for Mr Blackie's desk. Like the desk, this cabinet marks a change in Mackintosh's work towards a more sophisticated use of materials, often incorporating woods usually associated with traditional designs and used in these new pieces to emphasise the importance of the item's role in the design of the whole room. *In situ* (National Trust for Scotland). 1904.20.

tone for much of the work of the next few years. The Kingsborough Gardens armchair appears yet again in a slightly different guise at The Hill House: four were made for the drawing room, but all were painted black. Indeed, all the movable furniture for the drawing room is painted or stained black, while the fitted pieces are painted white. The large couch and the (now missing) easy chair are cubic pieces with an emphasis on broad, unmodelled planes relieved by simple incised decoration. In the hall, Mackintosh provided three sturdy, well-proportioned chairs which used the square as the major decorative motif. This was repeated in the hall table, where the oval top counters the more emphatic impact of the square.

These designs gradually drew Mackintosh to the opposite extreme from the Wärndorfer Salon furniture. As with much of the Willow Tea Room furniture, the emphasis on unmodelled surfaces and exposed grain gave an impression of sturdy utility. This might have been acceptable in a tea room, but Blackie obviously wanted something a little more elegant, something that would not be totally at odds with the white woodwork of his drawing room. Mackintosh's solution can be seen in the cabinet and writing desk, in both of which broad expanses of ebonised timber are set against subtle curves of glazed doors, inlays of coloured glass and mother-of-pearl, and discreet carved decoration. The decorative features, however, are not allowed to influence the basically linear design. Inlays, in particular, are confined to repetitions of geometrical shapes, mainly squares, with little or no reference to organic forms. The squares of mother-of-pearl both emphasise the rectilinear outlines and relieve the otherwise plain, flat surfaces of doors, legs and shelves. Incised squares in gables, and even a strange boss with overlapping inverted triangles on the cabinet complement the boxy shape of this furniture. The carving and inlays give the cabinet a grander appearance. Mackintosh gradually refined this new style over the next few years. In its severity of outline and massing, the new furniture was very different from the white-painted designs of 1902, but it could be softened by the use of other materials to produce a more sophisticated appearance.

In the following year, 1905, Mackintosh produced other designs for furniture for Blackie which applied the same principles in a slightly different

Circular table for the Director's Room, Glasgow School of Art (oak, stained dark). Probably designed as a table for meetings of the Board of Governors at the School. Certainly, they did not authorise any expenditure on the building between 1899 and 1907 unless it was for their use. Fourteen chairs were designed to accompany it. Glasgow School of Art. 1904.26.

Top left: Curved lattice-back chair for the Order Desk, Willow Tea Rooms, Glasgow (ebonised oak). One of the most impressive and novel of Mackintosh's chairs, it stood between the ground floor saloons, isolated and defining the point where the two rooms merged. The chequer pattern of the back takes the form of a stylised tree – another reference to willows. Glasgow School of Art. 1904.24.

Top right: Armchair with high back for the Director's Room, Glasgow School of Art (oak, stained dark). Two were made along with the twelve low chairs for meetings of the Board of Governors. Glasgow School of Art. 1904.27.

Bottom right: Armchair with low back for the Director's Room, Glasgow School of Art (oak, stained dark). Twelve were made for the School but others were either kept by Mackintosh or made for William Davidson. Glasgow School of Art; Hunterian Art Gallery, University of Glasgow. 1904.28.

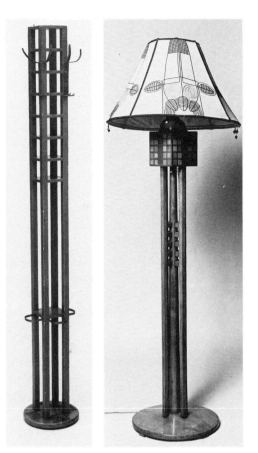

way. The lamp for the drawing room is unpainted and, apart from its elegant shade, relies for its effect on the manipulation of the grain of the timber. A pattern of squares is created, not by the use of inlays, but by transposing the direction of the grain between each square of wood and the next. This rigid but elegant pattern was not used again by Mackintosh until 1917 and 1919 when he designed some bedroom furniture for W.J. Bassett-Lowke. Its use in 1905 is atypical, and he seems to have been moved to offset the severity of the design with the apparently random placing of a piece of mother-of-pearl, almost like an ink blot, on the base of the lamp. At the same time, he made two more easy chairs for the drawing room. These are again made in ebonised timber, but this time are upholstered in a rich velvet.

The construction of the chairs lays great emphasis on the square-sectioned sticks of timber used in much of the bedroom furniture at Hous'hill. Here the sticks are paired, an oriental treatment that was repeated in the coupled columns and beams of the Library and Flower Composition Room at the Glasgow School of Art in 1909. Mackintosh has slung his upholstery across this framework of timber rails, which appear to be joined by dowelling pins. This apparently exposed construction and the use of timber rails fixed at right angles seems strangely prophetic of the furniture of Gerrit Rietveld. The Dutch members of De Stijl knew and admired Mackintosh's work, but no illustration of this particular chair was published at the time, and none of his other furniture used quite the same techniques of construction. However, Mackintosh was not totally honest in his construction, for the pins are not structural and perform no other function than mere decoration. But the principles behind the design, of luxury in the padded upholstery and more severe use of plain timbers in the structure, reflected the ideas first seen in the pieces of furniture designed in 1904.

Opposite page. Top left: Hat, coat and umbrella stand for the Room de Luxe, Willow Tea Rooms, Glasgow (mahogany, silver painted, with steel hooks and brass drip tray). Apparently designed some time later than the rest of the furniture for the Willow Tea Rooms. Glasgow School of Art. 1904.23.   The Hill House, Helensburgh. *Top centre:* Standard lamp for the drawing room (sycamore and mother-of-pearl, with embroidered shade). A design which, without its shade, could easily be taken for a product of the 1920s. Although the shade is firmly based on organic motifs, the stand itself is rigidly geometric in form and decoration, much of which is achieved by the manipulation and juxtaposition of contrasting grains in the timber. 1905.17.   *Top right:* Drawing room. An early photograph taken by a member of the family showing the new wall lamps and the standard lamp and armchair designed in 1905. 1905.C. *Centre right:* Square table (ebonised wood). A more complex, but on the whole less elegant, version of the table made in 1904 for the Blue Bedroom at Hous'hill. 1905.19.

Bottom left: Clock (ebony and stained sycamore, with ivory inlay and painted numerals). This simple design, a cube for the clockwork motor supported on 16 square columns, was modified and repeated in a series of clocks made for W.J. Bassett-Lowke c.1917-18. Mackintosh retained an example of the clock for his own collection. National Trust for Scotland; Hunterian Art Gallery, University of Glasgow. 1905.24. *Bottom right:* Easy chair for the drawing room (ebonised wood, with mother-of-pearl inlay and upholstered seat and back). A very different design from the other furniture at The Hill House, Helensburgh, all of which impose an upright posture on the user. The use of paired rails is more obvious here than in the contemporary square table. Mackintosh was to repeat the motif in a much larger format in his structural designs for the School of Art in 1907. 1905.20.

Hous'hill, Nitshill, Glasgow. *Top left:* Vestibule at Hous'hill, Nitshill, Glasgow. The square dominates the composition, repeated in the trellis for the plants, the pattern of the stone slabs and the door astragals. The flower stand (ebonised wood) is a domestic version of the garden lattice designed for Windyhill, Kilmacolm. Hunterian Art Gallery, University of Glasgow. 1904.A. Flower stand, untraced, 1904.32. *Top right:* Hall and staircase. The box lantern and the stencilling at the top of the stairs echo the arrangement of the hall at The Hill House, Helensburgh. The umbrella stand (wrought iron) is probably a version of the stands made for the Willow Tea Rooms,

Glasgow. The hat hooks demonstrate the delight Mackintosh took in creating abstract shapes in wrought iron. Hunterian Art Gallery, University of Glasgow. 1904.B. Umbrella stand, untraced, 1904.33. Hat hooks, untraced, 1904.34. *Bottom left:* Billiards Room. The screen around the fireplace ingle, with its rows of tapering posts, is a visual pun on the billiards cues. Hunterian Art Gallery, University of Glasgow. 1904.C. *Bottom right:* Dining Room. Although Mackintosh did not design the furniture, the stencilled decorations, lampshades and curtains are all his. Hunterian Art Gallery, University of Glasgow. 1904.E.

HOUS'HILL, 1904

Late in 1903 or early in 1904, Miss Cranston and her husband, Major Cochrane, invited Mackintosh to redecorate the interiors of their house, Hous'hill, at Nitshill, Glasgow and to design several items of furniture for it. Although Mackintosh apparently made no alterations to the outside of the house, he had an almost free hand inside and designed more furniture here than he had been able to for Walter Blackie at The Hill House. Miss Cranston lived at Hous'hill until about 1920, after which the property changed hands several times. It was eventually damaged by fire and was bought and demolished by Glasgow Corporation. The fittings were destroyed, but many items of furniture were sold at auction in Glasgow on 13th May 1933; since then, many of them have disappeared. The surviving photographs give a clear idea of the work done in 1904-05. Later stages, such as the Card Room of 1909, were not photographed.

The Hous'hill gives us, if anything, a better opportunity than The Hill House of seeing Mackintosh's skills and ingenuity as a furniture designer. Apart from the hall and billiards room, Mackintosh designed all the furniture for the drawing and music room and for two large bedrooms. All the furniture, except that for the drawing room, is more geometrical and severe than before, ranging from the extremely simple and rigid trellis in the vestibule to the more substantial and elegant wardrobes and cabinets of the Blue Bedroom. The fine hall dresser is in the style of the rather more luxurious pieces at The Hill House, but its effect is achieved by careful selection of grain in the timber and subtle arrangement of curves and lines in the design. It also places emphasis on the use of several squares to form a lattice, a feature used more frequently in later years, not only in furniture, but in the fittings of the larger rooms, particularly tea rooms.

Mackintosh paved the vestibule floor with stone slabs, apparently making wide joints covered with iron straps set flush. Some of the square slabs were incised with a floral pattern, which was taken up over the walls in the stencilled decoration of stylised roses and black trellis-work, a treatment that Mackintosh repeated in his own dining room at Southpark Avenue in 1906. Real flowers in pots or vases were arranged on a wooden stand, again in the form of a trellis, as the square was to be the dominant motif at Hous'hill. On the floor stood four gas-fuelled wrought iron lanterns, imitating braziers. The horsehair carpet that covered the hall floor and continued up the stairs was sewn to imitate a picture frame, with four pieces mitred together around a central rectangle, which was defined by a black band. The wrought iron hat hooks and umbrella baskets were rather more curvilinear than the severe hall dresser, a splendid composition of squares, solid and void, relieved by the gentle convex curve of a band of drawers along one of the shelves. The wall stencils, used high up on the staircase, recall the motifs

Billiards Room, Hous'hill, Nitshill, Glasgow, showing: the armchair (varnished oak); the high chair (varnished oak) – the raised seat gave onlookers a better view of the table; the billiards table; the billiards marking-board; the fireplace and ingle (stained wood) – two armchairs were placed beside the fire, hidden behind the screen of cue-like poles; the armchair (stained wood, upholstered) – one of two chairs designed to fit into the ingle next to the fire. 1904.D. All individual pieces are untraced. Armchair, 1904.37. High chair, 1904.38. Billiards table, 1904.41. Billiards marking-board, 1904.42. Fireplace and ingle, 1904.43. Upholstered armchair, 1904.44.

used at The Hill House, but each unit is larger and more elaborate. Again, the square is evident, but tempered by more organic shapes. The lantern, a series of simple metal and glass boxes, likewise echoes its counterpart at The Hill House.

Mackintosh's designs for a billiards room at The Hill House were never executed, and the one at Hous'hill is his only domestic rendering of a facility that was much in demand in Miss Cranston's tea rooms. Like the more public versions, it was predominantly dark, but it was definitely not as spartan. The embroidered curtains and pale patterned carpet relieved the sobriety of this gentleman's retreat, and the resulting atmosphere was more refined than that, for instance, of the basement rooms at Ingram Street. The table itself was decorated with applied squares of coloured wood or ceramic, and the conical shades over it had applied squares as decoration. The walls, which were divided by wide vertical straps, were covered with a dark paper to picture rail height. Where the rail passed across the window openings, it was inlaid with coloured glass to catch the light (a feature that was repeated in the studio at Southpark Avenue). No fixed benches were provided, but some of the chairs were raised on longer legs to give a better view of the table. The fireplace formed an ingle, with two armchairs screened from the rest of the room by a screen of tapering rods, a play on the shape of a billiards cue. The grate itself was of the usual simple wrought iron, here surrounded by cement inlaid with ovals of glass and inverted triangles of ceramic.

As at The Hill House, Mackintosh was not asked to design any furniture for the dining room, but he was responsible for the decorations, curtains and light fittings. The latter are very similar in pattern to the geometrical grid of the leaded glass fitting (a pre-Mondrian abstract composition) in the dining room at The Hill House. Here the fittings were used not just as a pair over the table but also as cubic wall lamps at the side of the fireplace and between the windows. The original intention was that these lights should have silk shades. As in all Mackintosh's dining rooms, the walls were dark, not panelled but covered with a dark paper stencilled with a floral design. A broad picture rail, stained black like the rest of the woodwork, divided this patterned wall from the white frieze above. Gauze-like embroidered curtains were hung from this rail as it spanned the window architraves; again, there were coloured glass inserts in the rail to catch the light.

The smaller of the two bedrooms that Mackintosh designed at Hous'hill, the White Bedroom, was virtually his last white room and the last occasion on which he used white enamel on his furniture. As at The Hill House, the white beds and bedroom fittings contrasted with the black chairs, which here had quite low backs. Although organic decoration was once more in evidence in the embroidered canopy and bedspreads and in the wall lamps, the furniture shapes were all definitely oblong or square and the decoration takes the form of pierced or incised squares. A new motif here, which is often seen in later pieces, is the tapering square knob on the bedside table; its black surface contrasts with the white enamel of the drawer, and it is itself decorated with inlaid mother-of-pearl. With the exception of the chairs, all the furniture from this room has disappeared.

Before Hous'hill, Mackintosh had always painted his bedrooms white, although some minor rooms at Windyhill and The Hill House had dark-stained doors and woodwork. In the Blue Bedroom at Hous'hill, white seems to have been used only for the walls and ceiling, and all the furniture was either ebonised or stained dark and waxed. Sadly, only five or six pieces survive out of almost twenty designed for this room; the bed, wardrobe, writing desk and couch seem lost forever.

Mackintosh made no attempt to alter or conceal the simple rectangular shape of the Blue Bedroom, and the furniture was all positioned against the walls, apart from the square table, which was isolated in the centre of the room; the only organically inspired decoration was the 'weeping roses' on the walls and the basket lamps. The furniture was all rigidly geometrical in design, with simple rectangular silhouettes, and its decoration took the form of squares, either incised or as inlays of coloured glass. Many of the

Above: Blue Bedroom, Hous'hill, Nitshill, Glasgow with the most elaborate bedroom furniture designed by Mackintosh: couch (stained oak with upholstered seat and back); double bed with canopy (stained oak, embroidered canopy); chair (ebonised or lacquered wood) – one of Mackintosh's simplest designs – a cubic seat with a back-rest of vertical and horizontal square rails forming a chequer pattern; dressing table chair (stained oak). Glasgow School of Art, 1904.J. Couch, untraced, 1904.68; double bed, untraced, 1904.70; chair, 1904.73; dressing table chair. 1904.74.

Below: Blue Bedroom, Hous'hill, Nitshill, Glasgow. 1904.K.

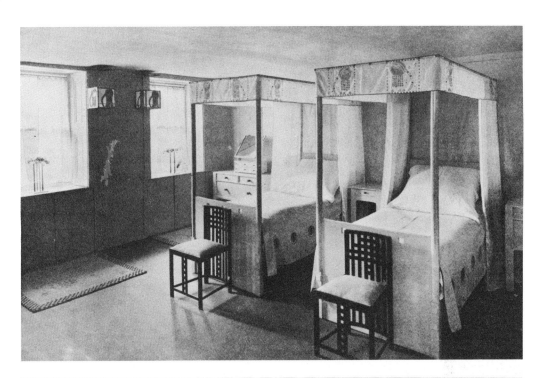

ideas developed in this room were used in later furniture and are as much a hallmark of a Mackintosh design as the white paint, purple glass and stencilled roses in his output between 1901 and 1903. Stretcher rails on dressing tables and washstands are arranged to form a lattice pattern; handles are

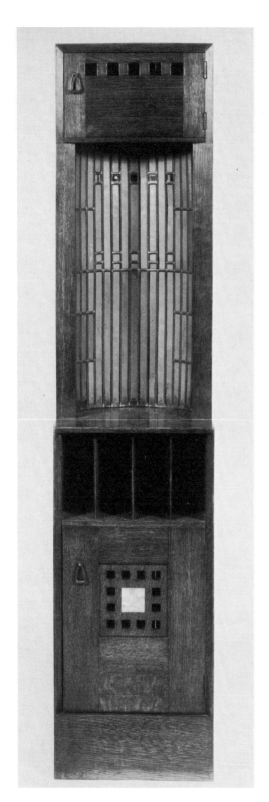

The Blue Bedroom, Hous'hill, Nitshill, Glasgow. *Left:* Cabinet (stained oak with a panel of leaded glass). Two free-standing versions of the bedside cabinets at The Hill House. A simple but very dignified piece of furniture. One remains untraced. 1904.67. *Top right:* Armchair (stained oak, with mother-of-pearl inlay and upholstered seat and back). A

recessed and backed with white metal or coloured glass; the timber is stained and polished smooth with wax to emphasise the grain, or ebonised with a black stain, again leaving the grain of the wood exposed. Sycamore, plane and maple were as likely to be used as oak, especially if the piece was to be polished. By selecting woods with a finer grain, Mackintosh was able to achieve finer details, sharper edges and thinner sections, the decoration often being solely the random variation of the wood grain itself. Thus the ebonised chairs from the White Bedroom at first glance appear rigidly and unimaginatively rectilinear. The aprons, however, have a delicate curve, and the back of the chair itself is curved across its width. Mackintosh also created a subtle pattern in the latticework in the back of the chair: the vertical and horizontal slats are cross-checked so that, seen from the front, the

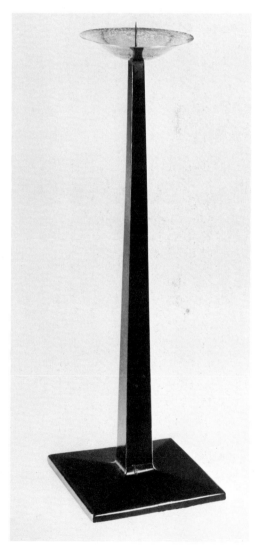

pair of these chairs was made to be placed either side of the fireplace. In plan, these chairs take the form of a faceted semi-circle but the segments which form the sides slope backwards as they rise, repeating the slope of the sides of the washstand and dressing table. 1904.81. *Opposite page. Bottom right:* Square table (stained oak with mother-of-pearl inlay in handle). The design is developed from the bedroom table at The Hill House but is rather more simply stated. It is, however, most successful in its handling of the diagonal stretcher and the subtle insertion of small square motifs. 1904.72. *This page. Left:* Dressing-table chair (ebonised or lacquered wood). An adaption of the bedroom chair, having a much lower back. 1904.74. *Right:* Candlestick (ebonised wood with silver cup).

Three were made for Hous'hill which are untraced, but Margaret Macdonald owned two identical candlesticks at her death in 1933, of which one survives. 1904.83.

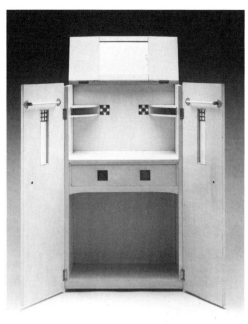

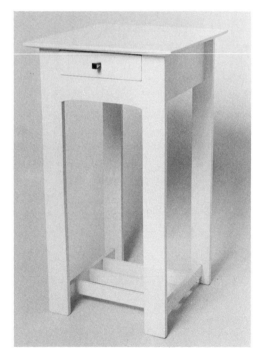

The White Bedroom, Hous'hill, Nitshill, Glasgow. *Top left:* Writing desk (wood, painted white, with panels of metal and coloured glass). The most elegant piece designed for this room, arguably the best of Mackintosh's white bedrooms. The Fine Art Society. 1904.85. *Top right:* Washstand (wood, painted white, with panels of coloured glass). An unusual design from Mackintosh where the bowl is hidden behind the closed doors of the stand. Two were made. The Fine Art Society; Royal Ontario Museum, Toronto. 1904.88.

Bottom left: Single bed (wood, painted white, with an embroidered or stencilled canopy). A very simple design, the only decoration (apart from the linen canopy) being three square holes pierced in the foot of the bed. Two were made. The Fine Art Society; Royal Ontario Museum, Toronto. 1904.89. *Bottom right:* Square bedside table (wood, painted white, with ebony and mother-of-pearl handle). Hunterian Art Gallery, University of Glasgow. 1904.90.

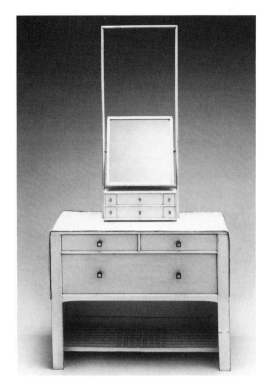 

The White Bedroom, Hous'hill, Glasgow. *Left:* Mirror (wood, painted white, with ebony and mother-of-pearl handles). These small dressing table mirrors were each placed on top of a set of six small drawers, the whole being positioned on top of the large chests of drawers in the room. Two were made. The Fine Art Society; Royal Ontario Museum, Toronto. 1904.91. *Right:* Chair (ebonised sycamore). A subtle design playing on the relationship of the straight pieces of timber which make the framework of the chair with the gentle curves of the seat rails and the back. The pyramid of frets in the back is enhanced by cross-checking the slats so that, when viewed from the front, the horizontal spars are unchecked, and from the back the verticals remain intact. Two were made. Four other chairs of a similar pattern but different dimensions are known which may have been made by one of Mackintosh's contractors without his knowledge or supervision. The Fine Art Society. 1904.93.

verticals are unbroken, with the grain running along the length of each rail, while on the back, the horizontals are dominant, cutting across each of the vertical rails.

Later tables followed the pattern of the Blue Bedroom table, with a square top and legs set on the diagonal; the paired diagonal stretchers were often joined by small bracing pieces to make a pattern of squares between the pairs of rails. The free-standing cabinets repeated the niches used on the bedside cupboards at The Hill House, but here formed an integral part in the design, their curves contrasting with the pierced squares and rectangular outline of the cabinet.

While the bedroom furniture at Hous'hill set the pattern for the future design of individual pieces, the drawing room points to a more considered and inventive manipulation of space. Mackintosh had always treated spaces in such a way as to express the function of a room. The bedroom and drawing room at The Hill House are both subtly divided by different ceiling heights or by variations in the windows to suggest specific uses for specific areas. The same techniques were used at the Willow Tea Rooms, the exhibition rooms at Vienna and Turin, and in the Wärndorfer Music Salon. At Hous' hill, in the later tea rooms and, above all, in the School of Art Library, spatial manipulation became even more expressive and complicated. Just as one must evaluate Mackintosh's furniture both as sculpture and as functional items for everyday use, so one should also acknowledge that his approach to spatial composition in these later works is primarily sculptural. Many of the later jobs involved internal alterations to existing buildings, and, given a restricting shell with a defined internal volume, Mackintosh could impose his character on the work only by creating ever more daring and ingenious arrangements of individual features such as screens, balconies and ornament. As sculptors release images from blocks of stone or wood, so Mackintosh manipulated the simple rectangular spaces of the rooms he was given to provide exciting vistas, subtle variations of light and texture, and powerful modelling of structural elements. The result was a series of expressive and dynamic interiors culminating in his masterpiece, the Library at the Glasgow School of Art.

The drawing room at Hous'hill was the main public room and served various functions, the various areas for which were defined quite precisely in the design. Mackintosh was faced with a simple rectangular space with windows on two sides, one of which was a semicircular addition. He may even have created this apse, but in any case he made use of the curve, echoing it with a second arc in the form of an open screen to create a circular space that served as a music room for Miss Cranston. At the opposite end of the room was the fireplace area, which was treated much as at Mains Street, Windyhill or The Hill House. The set of chairs around it were stained dark, unlike all the other white-painted furniture and woodwork in the room (except the piano, a traditional piece which had been decorated by George Walton). The open screen was a most effective method of dividing the room. Visually, it was sufficient to suggest a boundary when people congregated around the fireplace, but as it was entirely open, one could see and hear the pianist and other musicians through it on more formal musical occasions. Out of a somewhat amorphous room, Mackintosh created two distinct spaces that could be used as one when necessary. For the *Haus*

Hous'hill, Nitshill, Glasgow. *Opposite page. Above:* Drawing room. A view taken from the fireplace looking through the screen and showing the fitted cabinet, carpet and chairs. The chairs (probably sycamore or beech, stained dark, with inserts of coloured glass) are companions to the larger armchair. Although four were ordered and paid for only three were ever illustrated and only three have been traced. Mackintosh divided the cabinet (wood, painted white, with panels of clear and coloured glass and metal plates) into three horizontal sections, each contrasting with the others in a play on flat, concave and convex planes. The screen (wood, painted white, with panels of coloured and leaded glass, and candelabra of glass and metal) was almost semi-circular in plan and formed a visual break between the drawing room and the apsidal music room. It is a brilliant architectural device, both dividing the space into two separate parts and at the same time emphasising their spatial unity. Of all the losses incurred by the demolition of Hous'hill this is the saddest. Hunterian Art Gallery, University of Glasgow, 1904.G. Chairs, 1904.62. Cabinet, destroyed, 1904.57. Screen, destroyed, 1904.49. *Below:* Drawing room. A view of the fireplace (wood, painted white, with a cement or mosaic render inlaid with coloured glass). A simple structure drawing on the earliest fireplace at 120 Mains Street and The Hill House. The revolving bookcase (oak, painted white, with inlays of coloured glass). A fine design, each shelf having double the number of dividers of the one below, inset with small ovals of purple glass. 1904.I. Fireplace, destroyed, 1904.60. Revolving bookcase, 1904.52.

Hous'hill, Nitshill, Glasgow.
Above: Dining room. A view looking towards
the fireplace, flanked by bracket lamps
designed by Mackintosh. Hunterian Art
Gallery, University of Glasgow. 1904.F.

Right: Drawing room. This view shows the
furniture beyond the screen in the Music
Room, as this part of the drawing room was
called. George Walton painted the decorative
panels on the piano. The fitted seating (wood,
painted white, with upholstered seats and back,
and inlays of coloured glass and, possibly,
mother-of-pearl) continued the circle of the
screen. Also visible is one of two cabinets that
faced each other across the room at the point
where the wall began its semi-circular curve
towards the window (wood, painted white, with
glazed doors and inlays of coloured and leaded
glass). The cabinets incorporate a number of
ideas seen on other cabinets of this period, such
as the convex panels of leaded glass first found

on the bedside cabinets at The Hill House in
1903. 1904.H. Fitted seating, destroyed,
1904.50. Cabinets, destroyed, 1904.48.

eines Kunstfreundes, Mackintosh had given the option of two separate
spaces or one large room by providing removable screens between the
music room and the drawing room. At Hous'hill, the division is permanent
but transparent, creating a subtle ambiguity, an illusion of two separate and
finite spaces and, almost simultaneously, of one room contained within
another, with the two spaces flowing into each other and becoming one.

The window in the apse occupied one small segment of the circle's perimeter, and the rest was fitted with seating, not unlike that for Kingsborough

Gardens, curved to the profile of the wall, with two elaborate cupboards facing each other across the diameter of the apse. Where the open screen at The Hill House, dividing the hall from the lower landing of the staircase, had thick, square posts, the curved screen here is made up of a number of tall slats (about 10 cm. wide and 1 cm. thick) placed radially along the circle and secured between curved top and bottom rails. The top rail is a flat batten describing the perimeter of the music room at picture rail height. This wooden rail is reminiscent of the circular iron rail that Mackintosh suspended from the ceiling in the Front Saloon at the Willow Tea Rooms. The slats are spaced about 10 cm. apart, and shorter veins, each supporting an oval tray, were inserted at intervals. This device quickened the rhythm of the composition, which was further enhanced by the insertion of square or oval panels of coloured glass between the slats. Although Mackintosh had used screens before, none was as elaborate or as successful as this. He used a similar module in another curved screen in the Oval Room at the Ingram Street Tea Rooms in 1909.

The frieze and ceiling of the Hous'hill drawing room were painted white, but the walls beneath the picture rails appear from the photographs to have been a little darker. Small stencilled panels of roses were placed at intervals around the walls. The lighting took the form of a large, cylindrical leaded glass fitting in the music room, with a pattern in the leading made up of the rose and the square. Above each end of the fireplace was a wall-hung fitting of silvered metal and leaded glass, again featuring the rose; this fitting was repeated in the drawing room at The Hill House after the pendant lamps were removed in 1905-06.

Hous'hill, Nitshill, Glasgow. *Left:* Card table for the Billiards Room (varnished oak). The use of paired legs and diagonally crossed stretchers became a familiar motif in Mackintosh's later designs for tables. 1904.39. *Right:* Square table for the drawing room (perhaps oak, painted white). Two of these survive, one with its white paint intact bought at the Hous'hill sale in 1933, and another, stripped of its original finish and with no clear history, the latter in the collection of the Glasgow School of Art. The Fine Art Society; Glasgow School of Art. 1904.51.

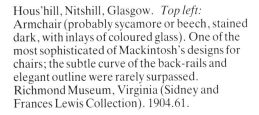

Hous'hill, Nitshill, Glasgow. *Top left:* Armchair (probably sycamore or beech, stained dark, with inlays of coloured glass). One of the most sophisticated of Mackintosh's designs for chairs; the subtle curve of the back-rails and elegant outline were rarely surpassed. Richmond Museum, Virginia (Sidney and Frances Lewis Collection). 1904.61.

Top right: Dresser for the hall (ebonised wood). A very simple yet elegant piece,

providing Miss Cranston with shelves to display her porcelain and deep drawers beneath. The design is severely rectilinear, relieved only by a curved band of drawers across the lowest shelf – a feature that a drawing indicates was possibly added at the client's request. 1904.35.

Bottom left: Oval tea table (sycamore, varnished). A more elegant version of the table at the Hill House, the legs being paired to improve both stability and appearance. Richmond Museum, Virginia (Sidney and Frances Lewis Collection). 1904.59.

Bottom right: Writing table (pine, dark-stained). It is not known for where this was made but the arrangement of the stretchers suggests that it is contemporary with the designs for Hous'hill. Glasgow School of Art. 1904.95.

SOUTHPARK AVENUE & COMMISSIONS, 1904-06

Hous'hill was Mackintosh's last domestic work of significance before the decoration of his house at 78 Southpark Avenue in 1906; it was also his last major domestic commission in Scotland (or indeed anywhere until Derngate in 1916). In 1904, he designed the chancel furniture for Holy Trinity Church at Bridge of Allan, near Stirling. This is more elaborate in its decoration than that designed for Queen's Cross Church in 1899, but the motifs are just as firmly based on organic forms. Such ornament appears sparsely on the low screen of light oak that Mackintosh placed in front of the organ, effectively defining the chancel. The pulpit, which is heavily decorated with carved tracery and supported on pierced legs, forms part of this screen. For the chancel itself, Mackintosh designed a communion table, an organ screen and at least one chair. The table is a more ambitious version of the one at Queen's Cross Church and, like it, is decorated with carved ovals, which

Pulpit for Holy Trinity Church, Bridge of Allan (oak). The church fittings, the communion table (oak) and organ screen (oak) at Holy Trinity show Mackintosh's version of medieval tracery and his expert knowledge of the skills of early craftsmen. The designs are based on floral and traditional lozenge motifs, similar to those in Gourock Parish Church. *In situ.* 1904.99. Communion table, *in situ*, 1904.100. Organ screen, *in situ*, 1904.101.

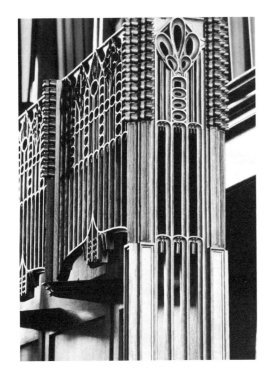

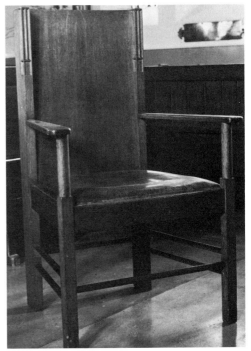

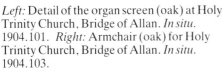

Left: Detail of the organ screen (oak) at Holy Trinity Church, Bridge of Allan. *In situ.* 1904.101. *Right:* Armchair (oak) for Holy Trinity Church, Bridge of Allan. *In situ.* 1904.103.

Opposite page. Above: Dining room for A.S. Ball, Berlin. Much of the furniture in this exhibition room for the German furniture store of A.S. Ball was based on the designs for the Room de Luxe at the Willow Tea Rooms of 1903-04. The small table (oak, stained grey-green) and the large table (oak, stained grey-green) are similar to the tables designed for the Room de Luxe, Willow Tea Rooms, Glasgow. The chair with the high back is identical to the high-back chair in the Room de Luxe, except that this one does not seem to have had the glass inserts or an upholstered back. Dining room, 1905.A. Small table, untraced, 1905.7. Large table, untraced, 1905.8. High-back chair, untraced, 1905.9. *Below:* Dining room for A.S. Ball, Berlin showing the sideboard (oak, stained grey-green, with panels of glass, ceramic or metal). The clock (oak, stained grey-green, with panels of clear and coloured glass) is a version of the one made for the Willow Tea Rooms, Glasgow. The chair (oak, stained grey-green) is identical, apart from a different arrangement of stretchers and the lack of upholstery on the back, with the dining chairs made for the Room de Luxe. 1905.B. Sideboard, untraced, 1905.5. Clock, untraced, 1905.6. Chair, untraced, 1905.10.

appear again in the organ screen, the most elaborately carved piece that Mackintosh ever designed. Combining Gothic tracery and fluted columns, it forms three canopies behind the communion table and screens the organist from the view of the congregation. Pendant panels in the centre of each canopy recall those in the gallery at Queen's Cross. Most of all, though, one is reminded of the carved pendants that Mackintosh designed for the School of Art Library in 1909; these use the same fluted oval as at Holy Trinity, but the motif becomes an end in itself, with subtle variations in each pendant. In the church, which is otherwise rather austere, the screen stands out as a rich and exuberant example of Mackintosh's inventive genius.

In 1905, a group of leading architects was asked to submit designs for furnished rooms for the furniture exhibition at the Berlin shop of A.S. Ball. The host architect was Alfred Grenander, and those chosen to exhibit

included Olbrich and Mackintosh, whose influence could be seen in most of the rooms and not least in the overall scheme put forward by Grenander; even Olbrich's dining room owed much to Mackintosh, although, unlike Mackintosh's entry, it was painted white.

Mackintosh's dining-room was L-shaped, with dark papered walls and with furniture based on the tables and chairs made for the Room de Luxe at the Willow Tea Rooms in 1903; the sideboard and dresser, however, are more rigidly linear and can be related to the Hous'hill Blue Bedroom and hall of 1904. The square is again the dominant feature of the scheme, with lattice work in the cupboard doors, pierced through the backs of chairs, or inlaid in ceramic or glass as in the sideboard and clock. It is a more severe design than any earlier dining room by Mackintosh except perhaps that for the *Haus eines Kunstfreundes* competition. He was not able to design the dining room furniture for The Hill House and Hous'hill, and at Southpark Avenue in 1906 he virtually recreated his 1900 design for Mains Street. The Ball dining room is therefore particularly important as the only domestic example of the genre designed *in toto* by Mackintosh between 1900 and 1916. The severity of the Ball dining room was repeated in the bedrooms designed for Bassett-Lowke in 1916 and 1917 and in the dining room for Bassett-Lowke's brother-in-law in 1919. This severity is not caused simply by excessive use of the square – the Dresdener Werkstätten bedroom of 1903 also stressed the square, but the overall effect was by no means austere. There, the squares were smaller and, as well as adorning the furniture, they were stencilled on the grey walls. The furniture at Berlin also has a strong horizontal emphasis in the wide shelves cutting across the broad expanse of timber in the upper part of the dresser, and in another wide shelf above the drawers. Even the table is larger than most others designed by Mackintosh, and the sideboard reinforces the horizontal feeling, being one of the few such pieces that is broader than it is high.

In the Oak Room at Ingram Street and in the Glasgow School of Art extension in 1907, Mackintosh had the opportunity to take this new style further, but nothing was as severe as the Ball dining room. Even in the Chinese Room at Ingram Street in 1911, the rigid lattice work was relieved by bright colours and by leaded glass in the square-framed partitions. For Bassett-Lowke, however, Mackintosh returned to this arrangement, and items like the Derngate dining room doors, the hall cabinet and chairs can all be traced back to the design for Ball.

In 1906, Mackintosh provided the Board of Glasgow School of Art with a new meeting room in what had been a ground-floor studio. (The previous Board Room, which had been provided in the east wing had apparently not been used by the Governors for very long, because lack of space had meant that it was needed as a studio.) Relations between Mackintosh and the Governors were rarely cordial, and this no doubt coloured Mackintosh's reaction to their commission for a new Board Room. They probably made it clear that they were expecting a room with a little more *gravitas* than the rest of the School and, judging by the results, they were prepared to spend more on themselves than on fitting out other rooms in the building. The new room had broad panels of polished timber divided by classical pilasters. These are fluted, with an idiosyncratic Ionic capital crowning each, but the top metre or so of fluting on each pilaster is decorated with an apparently random placing of squares and rectangles of timber flush with the raised lines of the fluting. As Thomas Howarth has observed, the result is like

Above: This august and classically-inspired space was created inside one of the ground floor studios in the School of Art. The furniture from the Director's Room was specially moved into it for this photograph. Royal Commission on the Ancient and Historical Monuments of Scotland, Edinburgh. 1906.A.
Below: Oval table for the Board Room, Glasgow School of Art (pine, stained dark). Glasgow School of Art. 1906.1.

musical notation and is the first example of a theme to which Mackintosh returned more successfully in the Library in 1909. Each of the pilasters has a unique arrangement of this strange decoration, which was repeated in the gallery pendants and the table legs in the Library. The Governors' reaction

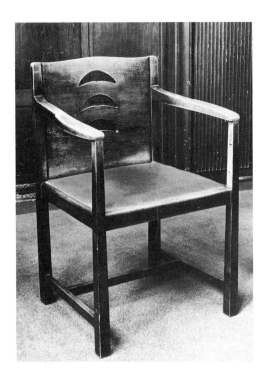

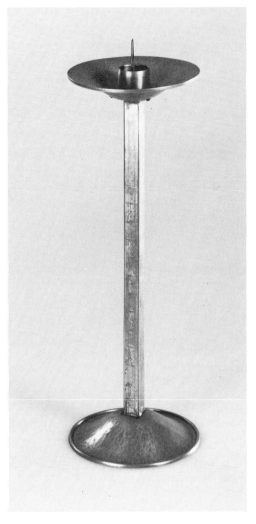

Left: Armchair for the Board Room, Glasgow School of Art (cypress). A more elegant version of the first Board Room chair designed in 1899, made in cypress and French-polished to harmonise with the new Board Room. Glasgow School of Art. 1906.2. *Right:* Candlestick with circular base (nickel-plated brass). The columns of these two candlesticks were originally diced but the decorative pattern has been virtually removed by constant polishing. 1905.31.

is not recorded, but John Burnet and John Keppie, both Governors at this time, are unlikely to have been amused.

In 1906, Mackintosh bought a house in the fashionable Hillhead district of Glasgow and left his flat at 120 Mains Street. The house overlooked the neo-classical Wellington Church and the grounds of Northpark House; it also had a view of Gilbert Scott's buildings for the University of Glasgow. 6 Florentine Terrace was the end house of a row, with a large gable wall facing south, while the main rooms faced east. Florentine Terrace was later assimilated into Ann Street (with number 6 becoming number 78); more recently, Ann Street was renamed Southpark Avenue.

Florentine Terrace was built in the 1850s. Its stone-built houses had bay windows on the ground and first floors, with a further floor and attic above. Externally, Mackintosh made few alterations, apart from the rearrangement of the windows, mainly on the south gable, and no amendments were made to the east front with the exception of the front door. The house originally had double storm doors, which folded back against the walls of a shallow porch; the main, inner door was half-glazed. Mackintosh removed the inner door completely and replaced the storm doors with a single, narrower door. The original opening was narrowed by the placing of a wide architrave at 45° to the door. The door was painted white and had a panel of four squares of purple glass; the architraves and the fixed light above were black. As a result of removing the porch, Mackintosh had also to narrow the hall, which he did by inserting two panels of butt-jointed pine planks (their joints hidden by a cover slip) on either side of the new door. These were attached at their west end to the walls, but were projected away from the walls at their eastern extremity so that the hall appeared to taper to meet the narrower door frame. The panelling was not continued on the walls of the hall, but Mackintosh repeated the arrangement of broad straps beneath a similarly broad picture rail that he had used in the drawing room at Mains Street. The picture rail was at the same height as the top architrave of the door to the dining room which, like all the woodwork of the hall except the front door, was stained black and waxed.

Nobody recalls the decoration of the hall clearly and no contemporary photographs survive. A photograph taken in 1933, however, shows that the staircase from the first to the second floor was wallpapered with a coarse grey or brown paper up to the level of the black wooden panelling on the west wall. This paper would probably have extended down to the ground floor and terminated at the panelling by the front door. The impression recalled by people who visited the house was of a dark hall relieved only by the window to the south and the white ceiling.

Although there is a standard Victorian panelled door from the hall into the dining room, it is not the original but was made for Mackintosh to the same height as the dining room fireplace that he had brought with him from Mains Street. The picture-rail connects the door and the fireplace. As the doors both of the room and of the press beside the fireplace were smaller in the other houses in Florentine Terrace, one must conclude that both were replaced by Mackintosh. As he had also kept the original window frames and the panelled shutters, he designed the two new doors to match the original woodwork. Mackintosh did, however, remove the moulded cornice, leaving a square junction between the walls and the ceiling. As at Mains Street, the dining room walls were covered in grey-brown wrapping paper, a small area of which has survived and shows that it was decorated with an all-over stencilled design of a black trellis with pink roses in the open squares. The frieze and ceiling were painted white, and three new electric lamps were hung down from the middle of the room.

The major alterations at 78 Southpark Avenue were at first and second floor levels. Originally there were two rooms on the first floor, and two doors on the landing. Mackintosh blocked the doorway to the first floor front room and opened up the wall between the two rooms to make a large L-shaped apartment. He designed a new door with a panel of heart-shaped inserts of purple glass and ran a broad plate from the architrave of the door to encircle the whole room. The front or eastern part became the drawing room, which was curtained off from the rear space, called the studio or the study, through which one entered. The original window on the south wall was blocked up by Mackintosh and replaced by a low, leaded glass casement that runs almost the full width of the south wall in the drawing room.

This was set in the frontal plane of the wall, which was almost 45 cm. thick, thus creating a deep shelf inside the window. The soffit of the opening was slightly higher than the picture rail, and Mackintosh inserted more squares of coloured glass into the rail so that they were back-lit by the new window.

On the east wall was a full-height, three-sided bay window flanked by another tall window similar to the one that he had blocked up on the south wall. To have made structural alterations to these would have disturbed the street elevation, but Mackintosh did reduce their internal height and thus the amount and quality of light that they admitted. He continued the picture rail across the tall window and boxed in the space above it. At the bay window, he carried the picture rail along the plane of the wall and built a new wall above the rail, blocking out the light from the upper part of the window. All the windows were covered with muslin, and Margaret's embroidered curtains hung from the picture rail, thus giving the impression – from the inside at least – that the windows in the room were all the same height, finishing level with the door and the picture rail. This elaborate arrangement had a considerable effect on the new room: the daylight came predominantly from the south and was warm in tone; the eastern light was filtered and softened by muslin; the room appeared much lower because of the continuous line of the picture rail and the deep artificial frieze newly created by the windows; the effect was reinforced by hanging the new electric lamps on long flexes so that they were level with the new rail.

In the back room, the studio, Mackintosh again carried his picture rail around the room, but he did not build a false wall across the west window. The reasons were both practical and aesthetic: the room did not receive a lot of light because the pitched roof of the rear extension was close to it and

78 Southpark Avenue, Glasgow.
Opposite page: The drawing room, looking west into the studio. Reconstruction at the Hunterian Art Gallery, University of Glasgow.
Left: The hall. The bench (1900.34) on the right was probably designed for use at 120 Mains Street. Opposite the window hung a mirror by the Macdonald sisters and Herbert MacNair. Photographed in 1962 before the interiors were dismantled. 1906.B.

Right: The dining room, looking west. Reconstruction at the Hunterian Art Gallery, University of Glasgow.

shaded it for much of the day; unlike the front windows, which were simple sashes without astragals and with transoms at about the same height as the picture rail, the rear window had small panes with several astragals, and the sash transom was below the height of the rail. To have blocked off the upper half would therefore have meant excluding a great deal of necessary light and would have resulted in an unsightly juxtaposition of sash transoms and picture rail. Mackintosh simply carried his broad rail across the window and inserted coloured glass into it to take decorative advantage of the extra light.

Both rooms were painted white; the moulded cornice in the drawing room (which, if it had matched the others in the terrace, would have been a Victorian extravaganza of fruit and leaves) was removed, but the more classical cornice of the studio was retained. The white fireplace from the Mains Street drawing room was transferred, with slight modifications to allow for the deeper chimney breast. However, the T-shaped grate was not repeated in the drawing room, and the irons and grate from Mains Street were used in a new fireplace in the studio. There are no reliable recollections of the appearance of the drawing room fireplace, which was altered in 1945 without a record being kept of its original appearance, but in all probability it was similar to those designed for Windyhill and The Hill House.

The fireplace in the studio was a simple wooden structure flanked by rather crude bookcases built into the recesses created by the chimney breast.

Electric light was used in both rooms, and the square metal fittings were slightly different versions of those made for use with gas at Mains Street. Although a wiring plan suggests that Mackintosh had intended grouping them again in clusters of four, there is no evidence that he ever used more than one fitting at each outlet (four in the drawing room, two in the studio).

On the second floor, the two bedrooms at the front of the house were joined together to form another L-shaped room. The fireplace from the Mains Street bedroom was transferred, as was most of the furniture. The washstand, which could only have been placed against the windows, was probably cut down at this time to prevent it obscuring the light. The artificial lighting was from the same square metal fitting that was used in the rest of the house.

From the second floor landing, a twisting staircase rose to an attic bedroom with French windows overlooking the University. The fireplace in this bedroom was identical with (if not actually the same as) that in the studio at 120 Mains Street. The most striking feature of this room was the decoration of the staircase that led up to it: the walls were painted with alternate black and white stripes 5 cm. wide, a form of decoration that Mackintosh returned to in the guest bedroom at Derngate in 1919.

The Mackintoshes left Glasgow in 1914 and closed their house, although they may have returned to it for short periods, either together or singly. In about 1919, William Davidson bought the house along with some of the furniture that had belonged to Mackintosh; he also brought with him some furniture from Windyhill. On Davidson's death in 1945, Glasgow University bought the house from his sons, Hamish and Cameron, who presented much of the furniture that had been used in it.

The University's intention was to open the house to the public as a museum. However, by the late 1950s, its plans for expansion involved the area of Southpark Avenue. Mackintosh's house occupied ground allocated in the University Plan to the new refectory, and demolition was inevitable. Andrew McLaren Young, Honorary Keeper of the University Art Collections and later Richmond Professor of Fine Art, drew up plans to incorporate the interiors in the new University Art Gallery designed by William Whitfield. As Mackintosh had made so few additions to the exterior of 78 Southpark Avenue, it seemed feasible to try to recreate his handling of the interior spaces inside a secure and air-conditioned building. Accordingly, the interiors were photographed, measured, dismantled and stored for more than ten years before being recreated inside a new concrete shell.

The old house was demolished, to an outcry from the admirers of Mackintosh's work and from those who viewed the University's encroachment on Hillhead with justifiable unease. McLaren Young bore the brunt of the blame, but his intentions were laudable, and few who criticised the University's actions bothered to check what the alternatives were to demolition and what the future held for the stored interiors. Hillhead was built on an uncharted warren of eighteenth-century coalmines with insecure workings

The bedroom, 78 Southpark Avenue, Glasgow. All the furniture, including the fireplace, was originally designed for 120 Mains Street in 1900. Reconstruction at the Hunterian Art Gallery, University of Glasgow.

and shafts. 78 Southpark Avenue, as the end house of the terrace, acted as a buttress to the others and was already beginning to show signs of subsidence. To have left the interiors there would have been folly; to have shored up the house would have been expensive; to have incorporated extra toilet accommodation and fire staircases to comply with building regulations would have ruined the interiors. McLaren Young's intention was not just to recreate the dining room and drawing room out of context, as his critics alleged; he had a site, an architect and a sympathetic University administration which would ensure that the final reconstruction would, if anything, surpass any improvement that could have been made *in situ*.

The site of the new Hunterian Art Gallery is in Hillhead Street, one block to the west of Southpark Avenue. The reconstruction of the house occupies the south-east corner of the building, giving it the same orientation and, because of the slope of the ground, virtually the same level as the original. The exterior is Whitfield's design, accepting Mackintosh's windows where they are required and perhaps paying some homage to Mackintosh. Inside, with the exception of the rear extension, the maid's room, the bathroom and attic bedroom, the reconstruction is complete on three floors. Panelling, doors, fireplaces, window sashes, even the balusters and handrail, are almost all original. Internally, the visitor is back in Mackintosh's own home, with almost the same views from the windows and the same furniture surrounding him. Perhaps the sceptics who doubted McLaren

Top left: Staircase at 78 Southpark Avenue, Glasgow. This photograph was taken in 1933 and shows the panel from the Willow Tea Rooms and the black-stained panelling below it. On the side walls can be seen a coarse dark paper which ends level with the panelling: this was probably used on the rest of the staircase and in the hall. 1906.G.

Bottom left: Dresser for the Dutch Kitchen, Argyle Street Tea Rooms, Glasgow (ebonised pine, inlaid with mother-of-pearl). A simple but bold design emphasising the square as a decorative motif. 1906.20.

Right: Chest of drawers for 78 Southpark Avenue, Glasgow (pine, stained dark, with aluminium-backed hand pulls). Glasgow School of Art. 1906.7.

Young's intentions or his powers of persuasion will react in the same way as Dr Thomas Howarth, who visited the reconstruction in the summer of 1977 before it was complete. He had not set foot in 78 Southpark Avenue for over twenty years, although he had visited it often in Davidson's time. In 1977, he saw little difference and, but for the bare plaster and paintwork, he felt he could have been back in the house he knew so well.

While 78 Southpark Avenue was Mackintosh's most important work during 1906, he also undertook one tea room interior and a domestic commission, Auchenibert. He was recalled by Miss Cranston to convert a square basement room in her Argyle Street premises to form a new tea room to be called The Dutch Kitchen. George Walton, who had been responsible for the decoration of the rooms designed in 1897, had now left Glasgow, and Mackintosh had total control.

Once again, he used the square as his theme, expressing it as a chequer pattern of differing sizes in black and white. This was relieved by the curved backs of the Windsor chairs and by the ogee curve of a wide, dark-stained

Left: Kitchen dresser for 78 Southpark Avenue, Glasgow (pine, stained black). A much more utilitarian design than the dresser for Miss Cranston of 1904; this piece stood in the scullery. Hunterian Art Gallery, University of Glasgow. 1906.8.

Right: Meat safe for 78 Southpark Avenue, Glasgow (painted wood). This rather crude piece of equipment stood in the yard outside the kitchen extension at 78 Southpark Avenue. Hunterian Art Gallery, University of Glasgow. 1906.10.

lintel that created an ingle by the fireplace. In the leaded glass panels of the false window openings in the south wall which filtered daylight from the pavement grids above, the square was replaced as a decorative motif by the rose. The floor was covered with black and white chequered linoleum, with half-sized squares in the fireplace ingle. Bands of white stencilled squares flowed down the black-painted central columns, which also served as hat-stands. The dado was covered in a small-scale chequer pattern, and even the dresser had square mother-of-pearl panels. Separating the fireplace ingle from the rest of the room was an open screen which supported the lintel; this screen, of tapering circular posts, was a larger scale version of the billiards room screen at Hous'hill. The curve of the lintel was echoed by that of the plastered fireplace, while the grate itself was set into a tiled wall with a concave curve; this curve was reversed in the front of the cement hearth, which thus had an elliptical plan. The wrought iron back panel of the grate was identical with that in the 1900 White Dining Room at Ingram Street.

Electric lighting was used, with pear-shaped hanging panels of coloured glass shading the pendant lamps. The effect was not as successful as with the bracket lamps at 78 Southpark Avenue. The daylight coming in through pavement lights must have been very soft, and the harsh electric light would have made the enamelled chairs sparkle. None of the movable furniture

Left: The Dutch Kitchen, Argyle Street Tea Rooms, Glasgow. The Windsor chairs are another Mackintosh version of a traditional chair, and like much of the furniture at the Dutch Kitchen, were enamelled green – the only occasion that Mackintosh used this finish. T.& R. Annan, Glasgow. 1906.I. Windsor chair, untraced, 1906.18. *Right:* The Dutch Kitchen, Argyle Street Tea Rooms, Glasgow. T.& R. Annan, Glasgow. 1906.J.

has survived, and the remaining fixtures are covered over by the fittings of the shoe shop that now occupies the premises.

In 1906 and 1907, Mackintosh was working on designs for Auchenibert at Killearn. This house, which was commissioned by F.J. Shand, is the least satisfactory of Mackintosh's domestic designs. The style, which can be described as Cotswold Tudor, was presumably used at Shand's request, for the result is not particularly happy. Externally, the battered chimneys with their widely projecting coping, the staircase bay, the polygonal bay to the drawing room and the wide leaded casements are the only indications of Mackintosh's hand in the job, which was completed by another architect, Hislop, after Mackintosh had resigned. Among the internal features, Mackintosh detailed the casements and leaded lights made by Henry Hope, the panelling made by John Craig for the dining room and morning room, hall staircase and upper landing, as well as the grates in the public rooms and bedrooms.

Shand's influence must account for the nature of the internal panelling, which is very simple, even severe, with classical details around the dining room fireplace. The pilasters flanking the fireplace are reminiscent of those in the 1906 Board Room at the School of Art, and the double *cyma recta* capital recalls the repeated motif in the Bridge of Allan church furniture. Certainly, the panelling is not what Mackintosh would have chosen to do if left to his own devices, and it is not surprising that he parted company with his client.

The staircase shows more evidence of his work, having similarities to the nearly contemporary staircase in the Oak Room at Ingram Street. A number of fireplaces also leave little doubt as to their designer, although they

Above: The dining room, Auchenibert, Killearn. This photograph, taken in 1973 like all the others of Auchenibert reproduced here, shows the panelling, fireplace and the wide casement. The latter is very similar – except for the stone mullions – to the window Mackintosh inserted in the south wall of his own drawing room at 78 Southpark Avenue. Hunterian Art Gallery, University of Glasgow. 1907.A. *Left:* Fireplace in the morning-room, Auchenibert, Killearn (pine, stained dark). Apart from the grate, the only Mackintosh feature in this room is the single carved panel over the mantelpiece. *In situ.* 1907.2. *Right:* Detail of fireplace.

163

Left: Door to the morning room, Auchenibert, Killearn. The linenfold carving on either side of the door repeats the motif from the fireplace. Hunterian Art Gallery, University of Glasgow. 1907.B. *Right:* Staircase at Auchenibert, Killearn. This photograph shows the balusters of the upper part of the main staircase which resemble those used in the Oak Room at the Ingram Street Tea Rooms, Glasgow. Hunterian Art Gallery, University of Glasgow. 1907.C.

are nowhere as elaborate as those designed for The Hill House, Hous'hill or even Ingram Street. Mackintosh was doubtless preoccupied with other matters: his move to Southpark Avenue, the extension to the School of Art, the Oak Room and The Dutch Kitchen for Miss Cranston were all executed during this period, and Mackintosh seems to have taken the line of least resistance with Shand. It is particularly unfortunate that this was so, as the house occupied a fine site, and even its exteriors could have been saved from mediocrity by a little more attention. Perhaps the fault was not all Mackintosh's, as he seems to have entrusted much of the detailed work to A. Graham Henderson, a draughtsman in the office whom he encouraged, as Keppie had earlier encouraged him. In this project at least, Henderson does not seem to have served Mackintosh well. Indeed, he later took the full credit for other jobs he had worked on (such as the Oval Room at Ingram Street), and finally bit the hand which had fed him by becoming one of Mackintosh's most severe critics and the source of many of the stories of office malpractice that were to damn Mackintosh in later years.

GLASGOW SCHOOL OF ART WEST WING & TEA ROOM DESIGN 1907-11

In 1907, Mackintosh started work on what was to be his greatest achievement, the Library of the Glasgow School of Art. He was also undertaking another job for Miss Cranston at Ingram Street, where he had decorated the main White Dining Room and the adjoining Cloister Room in 1900. Miss Cranston acquired adjacent premises on the corner of Miller Street in 1906-07 and asked Mackintosh to design new furniture and interiors for an extension, the Oak Room.

As the space was awkwardly tall and narrow, Mackintosh ran a balcony round three sides to provide extra accommodation for tables and to create the effect of the room being divided into a series of interlocking rectangular volumes. The balcony was supported on a row of square timber posts, each with a wide 'capital' at gallery level on which its joists appear to sit. As in the School of Art Library, the posts were carried through to the ceiling. Structural support was not needed for the ceiling, and the posts branched above the capital into five smaller square posts. These passed up through the front of the balcony, along which Mackintosh applied seven lengths of horizontal lath bent over the protruding posts to produce an undulating lattice effect.

This post and beam structure used with a wavy lath was repeated in the School of Art Library, with which the Oak Room has much in common, although Mackintosh was faced with much more serious spatial limitations than in the Library, which was undoubtedly a more successful composition. Nevertheless, the Oak Room has some interesting spatial arrangements within the existing structure, particularly around the staircase, which was defined by an open screen that also emphasised its importance as an element in the spatial handling of the room, breaking into the full-height void left by the three-sided balcony. The screen was composed of posts about 20 cm. apart linked by a series of square insets of blue glass at about waist height; below these insets, extra posts were inserted, quickening the rhythm of the screen, an arrangement similar to that in the Hous'hill drawing room screen of 1904. Stairs led down to the ladies' cloakroom and up to the balcony. On

Ingram Street Tea Rooms, Glasgow. *Top left:*
The Oak Room, photographed in 1971, before
the interiors were dismantled. 1907.D. *Top
right:* The Oak Room, in a photograph taken in
1971 showing the staircase screen against which
the sideboard was placed. 1907.E. *Bottom left:*
Details of carved decoration in the Billiards
Room. 1907.F. *Bottom right:* The Billiards
Room, Ingram Street Tea Rooms. 1907.F.

Left: Stool for the Oak Room, Ingram Street Tea Rooms, Glasgow (oak, stained dark). Although often called a 'waitress chair', this piece, of which 16 were made, is much more likely to have been for the use of the Tea Room's customers. The wavy top rail and twin wavy back rails echo the bent laths used in the Library at the School of Art and on the front of the gallery at the Oak Room. Glasgow Art Galleries and Museums; Glasgow School of Art. 1907.4. *Right:* Armchair for the Ingram Street Tea Rooms, Glasgow (oak, stained dark). Glasgow Art Galleries and Museums; Glasgow School of Art. 1907.5.

the rising flight, Mackintosh used his stud screen again, but the rails were seen full width rather than end on. They had a common top rail level with the floor of the balcony, and the studs did not have insets of glass but were pierced with oval holes. A number of decorative details in the Oak Room included ovals, some set into the timber panelling, some inlaid in coloured glass in the fireplace and others in mirror glass in the door.

Underneath the Oak Room was a second billiards room, entered through the earlier (1900) billiards room to the east. It was panelled with dark-stained pine and had a row of raised seating at each end. The north wall was inset with an elaborate glazed niche, which had a stylised tree carved from timber spanning its front edge.

Exact details of the furniture made for the Oak Room are not known, and only one drawing survives. The numbers of stools and armchairs listed in the job books cannot have filled the available space, and the surviving chairs must have been provided at or about the time that the room was decorated. These small chairs, which were probably referred to by Mackintosh as stools, have wavy top rails and back rails which echo the bent laths fitted to the front of the balcony and also used on the dresser.

The Oak Room probably suffered more than any other Mackintosh interior from the vandalism of the 1950s and 1960s. It was used for some

and in inset panels in the adjacent staircase. Glasgow Art Galleries and Museums. 1907.7. *Right:* Chair for the Oak Room, Ingram Street Tea Rooms, Glasgow (oak, varnished). A very sturdy chair which follows a fairly traditional pattern using chamfering on the rails, a motif repeated in the Library at the Glasgow School of Art. Glasgow Art Galleries and Museums; Glasgow School of Art. 1907.6.

Left: Sideboard for The Oak Room, Ingram Street Tea Rooms, Glasgow (oak with panels of coloured glass). The blue glass of the decorative panels was repeated in blue tiling on the walls

years as a souvenir shop, selling cheap Scottish mementoes to tourists. The proprietor evidently thought he could improve on the warm tones of the dark-stained oak panelling and proceeded to have it painted white and then applied artificial graining in a light oak colour which was varnished. The door was moved from the south to the north wall of the room, the fireplace was obliterated and the subtle open screen enclosed. The tiled walls at the servery in the south-east corner near the staircase were smashed or covered with grained plywood, and ugly electrical wiring and fittings were added. Modern acoustic tiles covered the ceiling; with their flecks of gold and silver, these were the final insult to Mackintosh. Rapidly advancing dry rot had taken hold of the panelling in the basement, where the fireplace had also been destroyed. As with the White Dining Room, all the remaining fittings were taken into store by the Planning Department of Glasgow Corporation and are now the property of Glasgow Museums.

In 1907, Mackintosh designed an extension for The Moss at Dumgoyne, near Killearn, but this has been demolished and only one indistinct photograph of it survives. Some kitchen fittings have been retained and follow

Top left: Doorway for the Lady Artists' Club at 5 Blythswood Square, Glasgow. Another of Mackintosh's plays on the classical language of architecture, intended here to complement the mid-Victorian architecture of Glasgow's grandest square. *In situ.* 1908.A. *Top right:* Detail of the doorway at the Lady Artists' Club. 1908.A. *Bottom left:* Square table for The Hill House, Helensburgh (lacquered sycamore, inlaid with mother-of-pearl). Based on the motif of a square, this table exploits the possible variations of solid and void within the overall cube of the table's shape. The mother-of-pearl is applied in small squares which are grouped together on the top to form four larger squares, each made of nine smaller squares; each side of the table is again divided into nine equal squares and each tier of the table is also of nine squares, some solid, some open. 1908.1.

the same basic pattern as the fittings in the service quarters at The Hill House.

The following year Mackintosh was commissioned to design new decorations for the Lady Artists' Club at 5 Blythswood Square in Glasgow, a job that was complicated by the Club's internal politics and was not completed to Mackintosh's design, at least as far as the drawing room was concerned. According to the published history of the Club, the staircase was wallpapered in dark brown, on which some sort of dark trellis stencil with touches of 'plum pink and silver' (probably similar to the dining room at 78 Southpark Avenue) seems to have been applied. A lattice-framed telephone box

Glasgow School of Art. *Top left:* Lecture Theatre. Royal Commission on the Ancient and Historical Monuments of Scotland. 1909.F. *Top right:* Architecture School. The architecture department was housed on the ground floor of the western extension to the School, in a space equal to three of the studios in the east wing. Royal Commission on the Ancient and Historical Monuments of Scotland. 1909.G. *Left:* Gallery of the Library. A view along the west side of the gallery showing the wagon-chamfering on the balusters around the window bays on the left. Royal Commission on the Ancient and Historical Monuments of Scotland. 1909.J. *Opposite page:* Life modelling room. A basement room, with its own roof-lights, projecting out to the south of the School. This was the room where Mackintosh devised a series of knot-like patterns for the end of the T-girders which supported the roof beams. Royal Commission on the Ancient and Historical Monuments of Scotland, 1909.H.

was incorporated in the hall, and Mackintosh produced one of his own neoclassical designs, not unlike the detailing of the Board Room at the School of Art, for the front doorway. In 1922, the wall decorations were covered over, and no trace of them now remains.

From late 1906, Mackintosh's main involvement was with the second phase of the Glasgow School of Art. The western part of the building, extending from the Museum to Scott Street was designed between September 1906 and May 1907. It is without doubt Mackintosh's greatest as well as his most famous work. The Renfrew Street elevation was continued in the same vein as the existing eastern bays, but the west wing was totally re-designed to produce a dramatic composition that contrasted totally with the east wing of the 1897 design. The interiors were completed in 1909, and the details would have been decided (if Mackintosh followed his usual practice) in the same year; certainly, much of the furniture for the library was not delivered until 1910.

The interiors followed much the same pattern as those completed in 1899, although a number of significant changes were made. An extra storey was provided to house classrooms, refectory and professors' rooms, which were linked by the 'hen-run', a wood and glass corridor suspended over the roof of the Museum, and reached by two extra staircases. Lectures were concentrated into one new theatre in the basement of the west wing (the 1897 drawings show this theatre as well as one in the north-east corner of the ground floor). The library was relocated from the ground floor to the first floor with a gallery and mezzanine above it.

The lecture theatre in the basement, adjacent to the west door in Scott Street, is panelled with stained timber. It is, on the whole, unremarkable, except for a sectional curved table and stage which can be removed piecemeal, and for the curved rows of benches with seats of such narrowness that generations of students have remarked on the lack of comfort. Outside the lecture theatre is one of the two new fireproof staircases introduced in 1907 – the other is fitted in the re-entrant angle of the east wing beside the old Board Room (since 1899, the School had had only one staircase, an incredible breach of fire regulations). Mackintosh varied the flat, smooth surfaces of the cement render on the staircases by introducing some decoration in the form of ceramic tiles. In the basement, oblong tiles are set vertically to embellish the corners of the walls, but for the landings he devised an arrangement of square tiles, playing off the coloured surfaces against blank squares of cement and never repeating any combination. At the top of each staircase, where the dividing wall between flights disappears,

Glasgow School of Art. *Top left:* West staircase. One of the two new staircases introduced in 1909 to provide a means of access to the new floor added above the studio roofs. As fire escapes they were rendered in cement to give a degree of fireproofing, a finish which has proved remarkably hard-wearing. The render follows the rise of the stair in a gentle curve and is decorated on each landing with groups of square tiles in different patterns. 1909.K.

Mackintosh placed a wrought iron grille terminating at the ceiling in an elaborate composition of trellis and curves.

The Library on the first floor was treated in a totally different manner from any other room in the School of Art. It followed the basic arrangement shown in the 1897 drawings, with a gallery over the main floor, a repetition of the design for the Museum in Queen Margaret Medical College, which dates from 1895. Many of the individual motifs with which Mackintosh had experimented in the period 1904-07 were brought together in the library in a single harmonious design. It is Mackintosh at his most inventive, but he does not lose control of his inspiration, and the final composition is one of his most ingenious and, at the same time, most controlled works.

Mackintosh created the Library by fitting three floors in the west wing into the same height as one of the first floor studios. The top floor of the three provides a book store and is suspended on steel stirrups from the main east-west beams that support the second floor of the wing. By diverting the enormous weight of the book store so that he did not have to provide a substantial stucture below to support it, Mackintosh was able to give a very open treatment to the main part of the Library. In fact, his interior handling of the space was subjected to only one structural restraint: the position of the two main east-west beams which supported the weight of the Library. He positioned three oriel windows on the west elevation, separated by the beams, and these windows rise the full height of the Library and its gallery and also light the book store above. The window end of the gallery is shaped to complement the three sides of the windows, thus forming hexagonal wells; the hexagon was repeated in the book store, where it was completed by the internal glazed lattice windows.

To support the gallery, Mackintosh had to place his columns over the main beams, just as he had proposed in his original 1897 plans for the School. His major change to the early plans was a stroke of genius: he narrowed the width of the gallery, thus dramatically improving the appearance of the library by creating a larger central well and also requiring the beams supporting the gallery to be pushed out beyond it to meet the fixed main posts.

Opposite page.
Bottom left: The loggia. Much of the new work on the top floor was carried out in brick, which was left exposed. This loggia formed a corridor, connecting with the 'hen-run' over the roof of the Museum with the west staircase. The professors' studios are on the right and the windows on the left have a panoramic view out from Garnethill and over Glasgow. 1909.M.
Top right: The Library in 1910, before the delivery of the tables and the magazine rack for the periodical table. This photograph clearly shows the structural lines of the room, with the columns aligned on the beam which crosses the room from the west window to the east wall. Set back along cross beams which flank the main columns is the gallery which runs completely around the Library. 1909.I.

This page. Left: Composition room, formerly the flower-painting room. The arrangement of paired beams, crossing each other at right angles recalls some elements of Japanese construction. 1909.L. *Right:* The refectory. Referred to in Mackintosh's plans as the 'Diploma Studios', it was built on top of the studios of the east wing in 1907-9. The long windows on the left look out over the Renfrew Street but are hidden behind the projecting eaves of the roof of the 1899 building. The timber structures on the south wall are the ventilation ducts from the lower floors which exhaust to the roof. Royal Commission on the Ancient and Historical Monuments of Scotland. 1909.N.

Above: Writing desk (ebonised cypress) for the Masters' Room, Glasgow School of Art. Only the professors had individual offices or studios and the other members of staff shared common rooms. This desk was used in the Masters' Room and provided accommodation for three teachers. Glasgow School of Art. 1910.3.

Opposite page: Periodical desk for the Library,

Glasgow School of Art (cypress, stained dark, with inserts of coloured glass). The upper structure, which provides racks for magazines, is simply slotted on top of the desk and is held in place by a system of exposed wedges. The carved panels on the end of the desk are all random patterns like those on the legs of the tables and on the gallery pendants. Glasgow School of Art. 1910.5.

This structure was an extremely elegant solution and one on which he could place a strong sculptural emphasis; he thus created an exposed construction that was perfectly functional and did not require any additional ornament.

The broad posts that rise from the floor are divided into three parts at gallery level; the central section of each rises to the ceiling, while the two outer posts turn through an angle of 90° to become the beams that support the gallery, the front of which is set back so that the arrangement of the twin beams is clearly exposed. None of these structural elements received any applied decoration – the beauty of the structure, the materials and the detailing providing all the decoration that the framework needs.

However, the library is not a plain room. Although the framework of the exciting new space was left unadorned, other surfaces were treated in a more decorative manner. As if to emphasise the distance between the main posts and the gallery front, Mackintosh placed three square balusters along each pair of beams; the corners of these balusters are scalloped (or wagon-chamfered), with the curved surfaces painted in bright red, green or white.

At the top of the gallery front, a bent lath is applied, as in the Oak Room, and its wavy line is repeated in another plane in a beam running above the

gallery, the only curved element in a ceiling that is otherwise of a bold, simple lattice construction. The wave also appears on a much larger scale in the ogee curves of the aprons of some of the bookcases. The lath on the front of the gallery bends over a series of panels fitted to it. The treatment echoes that of Queen's Cross Church in the way that alternate panels project down below the level of the gallery floor. As at the church, Mackintosh pierced the pendant panels, but here the pattern on each is different, a play on fluting and ovals not unlike the pilasters in the Board Room of 1906. All the woodwork, including the ceiling, is stained deep warm brown like that originally used in the Oak Room.

The ingenious pattern of fluting and ovals is incorporated in the stretchers of the periodical desk and the legs of the tables designed for the library, but nowhere is exactly the same combination of pierced holes repeated. The furniture for the library comprises only four or five designs – apart from the periodical desk and the tables, there are Windsor chairs, (similar to those used at The Dutch Kitchen) for the readers, another magazine stand, possibly used in the mezzanine store, and circular newspaper racks, which may even have been designed in 1899. There appear to have been no special fittings designed for the Librarian's office or for the gallery, access to which was gained via the new escape stair rather than by the turret stair shown in the 1897 design (the present internal staircase at the side of the Librarian's office is a more recent addition).

The lighting also contributes to the spatial effects in the Library, with pools of light concentrated in the gallery, over the tables beneath it, and in one central flood of light over the periodicals table. Mackintosh's ingenious

Glasgow School of Art.
Top left: Table (ebonised pine). Probably designed for use in the Library or Museum at the Glasgow School of Art. 1909.22. *Bottom left:* Newspaper racks for the Library (pine stained dark). Glasgow School of Art. 1910.7. *Top right:* Side table with wavy edge for the

Director's Room (cypress, stained dark). The wavy pattern along the edge of the table top and the lattice grid on the stretchers are two commonly used motifs at this period. Glasgow School of Art. 1910.1. *Centre right:* Square table for the Library (cypress, ebonised or stained dark). A simple sturdy design for the

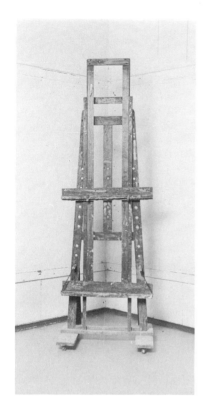

Opposite page.
Bottom right: Magazine stand (pine, stained dark). Probably used for the display of large volumes of newspapers, although it is possible that it was designed for use as a stand for drawing boards, with the central zinc-lined well filled with plants for botanical sketches. 1910.6.

This page.
Top left: Easel for the Glasgow School of Art (wood, originally varnished). An exaggeratedly tall design which complements the vast spaces of the painting studios. 1910.
Bottom left: Windsor chair for the Library (pine, varnished). A more elegant version of the Windsor chair which Mackintosh designed for the Dutch Kitchen in 1906. These chairs, however, proved unable to withstand the rigours of constant use by the School's students and most of them had to be reinforced with steel rods before being withdrawn from general Library use. 1910.9.
Right: Dresser for the Ladies' Common Room (cypress, stained dark). Mackintosh's version of a traditional dresser/bookcase, making much use of the curved or scalloped edging which was used at the Oak Room in 1907 and the School of Art Library in 1909. 1910.12. All Glasgow School of Art.

use of readers in the Library. All of these tables (ten survive) have panels of open carving on their legs, each panel having an apparently random arrangement of the same oval motif which is used on the pendants of the gallery front. Like the pendants, no two of these panels are the same. Glasgow School of Art. 1910.8.

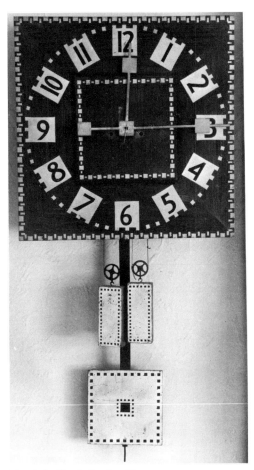

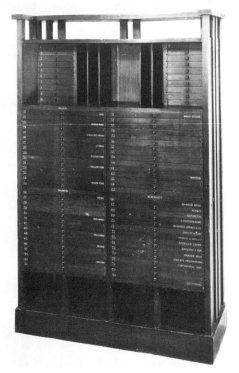

Top left: Clock for the Glasgow School of Art (wood, with stencilled numerals). Glasgow School of Art. 1910.11. *Centre left:* Sample cabinet for William Douglas (sycamore, stained dark). Douglas was a decorating contractor and a friend of Mackintosh, who designed a number of pieces for his home. This piece, however, was very much intended for the office, being very simple and workmanlike in design and construction. Glasgow School of Art. 1910-12.23. *Bottom left:* Pembroke table for William Douglas (oak, with chequer decoration with leaves down). It is unusual to see chequer

decoration applied to a piece of furniture, although it was a frequently used motif in Mackintosh's schemes for wall decoration. 1910.21. *Top right:* Clock for William Douglas (oak, stained dark, with stencilled decoration on face, weights and pendulum). A clockwork version, with weights and pendulum, of the electric clock designed for the Glasgow School of Art. 1910.20. *Bottom right:* Pembroke table for William Douglas with leaves up. 1910.21.

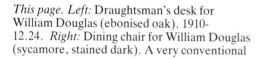

This page. Left: Draughtsman's desk for William Douglas (ebonised oak). 1910-12.24. *Right:* Dining chair for William Douglas (sycamore, stained dark). A very conventional chair in appearance but somewhat more sturdy than many Mackintosh chairs. 1910-12.25.

down-lighters control the spread of light, creating an alternating pattern of light and shade, which enhances the rhythm of the decorations.

On entering the library for the first time, many people are surprised by its intimate scale, especially if they already know it from photographs (which have usually been taken with a wide-angle lens). It is quite small room, only 11 metres square, but by skilful manipulation of the space, Mackintosh has created an open, airy room which continually surprises even the habitual user with new vistas and rediscovered details.

Mackintosh's remaining jobs in Glasgow were almost all for Miss Cranston. In 1909, she and her husband invited him back to Hous'hill to do some further work including the design of furniture and fittings for a new card room. No photographs of it survive, and we are dependent for our knowledge on the few remaining drawings and the details in the job books. The drawings are for the chairs, tables and fireplace; they give little indication of the layout of the room. The tables seem to have been quite elaborate, with a complex arrangement of stretchers and a folding top

Chair for the Card Room, Hous'hill, Nitshill, Glasgow (beech, stained dark and polished). A rather contorted version of a traditional Windsor chair; sixteen were made but only one has been traced. 1909.4.

Table for Hous'hill, Nitshill, Glasgow (cypress, stained dark, inlaid with ebony and mother-of-pearl). A unique and sophisticated design, miniaturising some of the elements of the Library at the Glasgow School of Art into a writing table. The paired beams of the Library are echoed in the legs and the chamfering of the balusters and the wavy lath around the balcony are repeated in the rails below the drawers. Glasgow School of Art. 1909.11.

which extended to provide a larger playing space. The decoration of the room was apparently based on the use of such dramatic elements as gold leaf for the walls, enriched with four gesso panels by Margaret Macdonald entitled *The Four Queens* and an extensive use of plate glass in the fireplace. The room might well have been similar to its contemporary, the Oval Room at Ingram Street.

The two new rooms completed at Ingram Street in 1909-10 were claimed by A. Graham Henderson as his own design. In 1910, Henderson was one of Mackintosh's draughtsmen and was possibly responsible for producing some of the working drawings for the Oval Room, but certainly not for the design.

The area in which Mackintosh created the two new rooms at Ingram Street was a narrow rectangular space south of the Oak Room. Each room had a bow window through which a grey light from the internal courtyard could filter, but there the similarity between the two ended. The upper room, the Oval Room, was a mezzanine at the same level as the Oak Room balcony which gave access to it; it probably functioned as a smaller and more intimate tea or coffee shop. The east window was a bow and was broken up by many astragals into a latticework of small square panes. To its right, the fireplace had a cement surround, and the walls of the room were divided into narrow, canvas-covered panels by thin straps. Although the overall impression of the room was of an oval, it was by no means that simple. The basic oval was continuous only at a high level in the room, and even then it was broken by two shallow projections on each of its longer sides. At the west end, the line of the oval was carried through an open screen, which was very similar to that at Hous'hill, but without the inserts. This screen admitted light from the Miller Street windows, but effectively hid the patrons from the sight of those in the Oak Room below.

The Oval Room had several affinities with the music room at Hous'hill, as it took a curved form (which at Hous'hill had been a circle rather than an oval) but had the line of the curve broken by recesses and projections. At Hous'hill, the cabinets and seats varied the outline of the circle described by the screen, but all the different curves were concentric. Here, the walls formed curved recesses outside the line of the oval (as seen at ceiling level) or projected into it; these shallow projections contained niches, again like the cabinets in the Hous'hill room. Even the bow window took a different line from the basic oval, the shape of which was retained in a narrow bank of canvas panelling above the window. It was a complex room, and Mackintosh possibly tried to fit too many subtle variations into such a small space. It is difficult to know, though, how the room would have appeared on its completion. The original colour schemes have long since been painted out, and the layout of the furniture was never recorded. In fact, the only photographs of the Oval Room and the Ladies' Rest Room were taken in 1971, when they were being dismantled.

The Ladies' Rest Room on the ground floor had the line of the Oval Room above imposed on it by the free-standing columns which support the mezzanine floor. Basically, however, it is a rectangular room with dark-stained panelling, provided with a series of recesses for couches and other

Fireplace and bow window for the Ladies' Rest Room, Ingram Street Tea Rooms, Glasgow. Photographed in 1971. This room, and the Oval Room above it, were fitted into a space at the back of the Oak Room. In both rooms Mackintosh makes much of the relationship between the overlapping ovals of the plans of the rooms and their relationship with the basic rectangular space in which each is contained. 1909.A.

Ladies' Rest Room, Ingram Street Tea Rooms, Glasgow. Photographed in 1971. The columns support the Oval Room above. 1909.B.

Fireplace and bow window, Oval Room, Ingram Street Tea Rooms, Glasgow. Photographed in 1971. 1909.C.

Left: Ingram Street Tea Rooms, Glasgow. Oval Room, photographed in 1971. The screen of flat vanes at the end of the room recalls the screen in the Music Room at Hous'hill of 1904. 1909.D.

Right: Chair (wood, stained dark, with inserts of coloured glass). Two chairs were made for the Ingram Street Tea Rooms in 1909 which remain untraced. They each cost £7.5.0d, a considerable sum for a single piece of Tea Room furniture which suggests that they must have been quite elaborate designs. The only known chair which possibly fits the description is a chair, now lost, which was lent to the Mackintosh Memorial Exhibition in 1933. Its size and shape, segmental in plan, suggests that it was used in the Ladies' Rest Room as the vanes in the upper part of the chair repeat the open screen at the end of the room. Untraced. 1909.17.

furniture. Adjacent to the window, which admitted very little light, was a fireplace with a gold mosaic surround. The west end of the room was open to the Miller Street elevation of the Oak Room, which had full height windows, but little light from them would have reached the Rest Room because it would have been blocked out by the shadow of the mezzanine floor above. The design for the Rest Room seems less successful than that for the Oval Room.

In 1911, Mackintosh produced three more tea room designs. One of these was for the White Cockade Tea Room at the Glasgow Exhibition. No informative photographs exist of this temporary tea room, and only a single drawing has survived. The job book suggests that it had internal panelling similar to that used later in the year in the Chinese Room; other entries imply that the pay desk was transferred to Ingram Street for use in the Chinese Room. It is possible that the large quantity of wavy-backed chairs

Ingram Street Tea Rooms, Glasgow. *Left:* Chair with a wavy back splat (oak, stained dark). Glasgow Art Galleries and Museums; Glasgow School of Art. 1909.14. *Right:* Table (oak, stained and waxed). The scalloping and the chamfering used to produce an undulating line is typical of much of the work of this period. What these tables were used for is still uncertain; perhaps it was for the storage of magazines and papers in the Ladies' Rest Room. Whatever it was, it must have been a purpose which brought the tables into contact with the patrons of the Tea Rooms as the table is a much more exciting design, and cost much more than almost any other table in the whole of Mackintosh's work for Miss Cranston. 1909.13.

were made for this tea room and later transferred to Ingram Street; only 28 were required for the Oval Room, but another 29 survive, and there is no record of such a large number of chairs being made specifically for any other room at Ingram Street.

The two rooms designed for Ingram Street in 1911 show that Mackintosh's powers of invention were not failing, even if his ability to attract new commissions had begun to wane. In the Chinese Room and the Cloister Room can be seen elements of the special form of modernism that is apparent in the Library at the School of Art. The crispness of detail in the Library and the novel solution it offers to the problems posed are modern in approach, though not, as Thomas Howarth notes, revolutionary in intent. In these two rooms for Miss Cranston, Mackintosh went further than he had in the Library, laying the foundations of the style he perfected at Northampton five years later. This new style, though virtually ignored by the following generation, solved the persistent problems of the modern use of decoration in a simple and quiet manner without the dogmas of the Arts & Crafts movement or the polemic of the protagonists of the Bauhaus and the International Style.

205 Ingram Street does not appear to have been worked on by Mackintosh before 1911, when it was turned into the Blue or Chinese Room. Mackintosh left the original, rather ugly ceiling in place, but painted it dark and then screened it from view using a series of horizontal lattices painted bright

The Chinese Room, Ingram Street Tea Rooms, Glasgow. *Above:* Photographed c.1950 before the central lattice screens were removed. The lights and the arrangement of the fitted seating and wall panels can be clearly seen. Hunterian Art Gallery, University of Glasgow. 1911.A. *Below:* Detail of the door canopy. Hunterian Art Gallery, University of Glasgow. 1911.C.

painted blue, Mackintosh here used a black lacquer – another Oriental technique – for these chairs. Glasgow Art Galleries and Museums; Glasgow School of Art. 1911.4.

Bottom left: Domino table for the Ingram Street Tea Rooms, Glasgow (ebonised oak). Possibly made for use in the Chinese Room. Glasgow Art Galleries and Museums; Glasgow School of Art. 1911.5.

Right: Cash desk for The Chinese Room, Ingram Street Tea Rooms (wood, painted blue). The twin themes of lattice panelling and Chinese carved decoration are combined in this very individual design. Glasgow Art Galleries and Museums. 1911.3.

Top left: Chair for The Chinese Room, Ingram Street Tea Rooms, Glasgow (lacquered sycamore). The fretted back and side rails match the Chinese-style motifs of the room; unlike the woodwork, which was mainly blue like most of the woodwork in the room. These lattice screens were supported at the walls on projecting panels of lattice construction and in the centre of the room by free-standing lattice screens. Between the projections, the walls were covered with a heavy blue-painted canvas, over which more lattice-work was applied.

The central screens had tall posts at each end rising above the horizontal screens; at the top of each post was a pagoda-shaped sculpture. Other identical structures were suspended from the ceiling through the voids in the lattice, and beneath them were hung light shades. At the door stood a large square pay desk, which also supported the overhead screens, and at the south end of the room a timber and mirror glass screen partitioned the area from the servery and the ante-room to the Cloister Room. Over the doorway in this screen, Mackintosh devised an elaborate canopy of fretwork in the Chinese style.

In contrast to the refurbished Cloister Room designed later in 1911 and opened in 1912, the Chinese Room is severely rectilinear. The emphasis is wholly on the square and the relationship between the solid and open panels of the lattice-work. This linear style is relieved by the fretwork decoration of the door canopy, the chairs, coat-hooks and pay desk, and by the treatment of the lattices that project from the wall; these are composed of open panels about 20 cm. deep, and the spaces between the lattice frame are filled with concave niches of leaded mirror or coloured glass, or sheets of a plastic substance, or simple flat leaded glass panels. Curved niches were used in many fittings and pieces of furniture from about 1903, but the material used to decorate them was usually coloured glass. Mackintosh's use here of one of the new casein-based plastics, Lactolith or Galalith, is the first recorded instance of his using a synthetic material in place of glass. It is interesting to note that he used it only in sheet form, not taking advantage of the fact that it can be moulded to return to the more sculptural style of 1902.

One of the most striking features of the Chinese Room was its use of colour. The fittings were apparently painted in bright blues and reds, a new element in Mackintosh's work. At the School of Art, the colour had been very restrained; although there is more in the Library than elsewhere in the building, it is still restricted to the scalloped edges of the balusters in the gallery. Apart from white paint, colour was normally used by Mackintosh only in dabs of intense hue such as the glass inserts in furniture, in the pastel colours used in upholstery or ornament and in the stencil decorations he designed for many of his domestic commissions. At the Willow Tea Rooms, there was a more conscious attempt to make greater use of colour, particularly in the silver and purple of the Room de Luxe. But before 1911, the colour was always very carefully controlled and restricted. In the Chinese Room, this policy was abandoned in one of the most 'modern' gestures that Mackintosh ever made. Later in the year, in the Cloister Room, he returned to a more controlled, but still extensive, use of colour.

The Cloister Room was a small rear tea room that Mackintosh had previously decorated in 1900; it linked one of the original rooms decorated by Scott Morton in about 1899 with the Chinese Room. Although no furniture seems to have been designed specifically for it in 1911, the alterations made to the room itself were more extensive and elaborate than in any of the other rooms at Ingram Street.

The ornate plaster ceiling and frieze were hidden by a new and lower barrel-vaulted ceiling of fibrous plasterwork. Three deep 'domes' in this vault accommodated ventilation grilles and light fittings. The rest of the ceiling was smooth except for raised bands of diaper pattern which spanned it about every 1.5 metres. These bands imitate in low relief the wagon-chamfering used on the balusters in the School of Art Library and related to the pattern that Mackintosh designed for the walls; they were placed above flat wall panels, and where the ceiling was smooth, the walls below were raised in a pattern of superimposed panels, so that the rhythm of smooth and raised panels on the ceiling was reversed on the two long walls. The wall panels were of plain waxed timber decorated with strings of painted diapers in red, green and blue, outlined in black. These strings ran vertically in pairs to divide the flat panels and also defined the edges of the super-imposed panels, each of which was smaller than the one beneath, making a shallow projection into the room. The effect was something like that of the superimposed orders of a Romanesque doorway. At the junction of wall and ceiling, a horizontal cornice of painted diapers ran the full length of the long walls. Mackintosh retained the open screen he had designed in 1900 for the east end of the room, but at the west end he divided the wall into ten equal panels. The central two formed a single niche backed with leaded mirror-glass strips and crowned by an elaborate canopy made of strips of wood, each with its leading edge scalloped or chamfered; the strips were arranged one above the other so that the concave scallops contrasted with

The Cloister Room, Ingram Street Tea Rooms, Glasgow. Photographed before being dismantled in 1971; the panels of leaded glass in the foreground are not by Mackintosh. 1911.D.

Above: Table for William Douglas (mahogany, French-polished). An elegant and complex arrangement of the legs transforms what is otherwise a simply stated design. 1912.3.

Below: Garden seat for The Hill House, Helesburgh (pine, stained dark). *In situ* (National Trust for Scotland) 1912.1

convex chamfering on adjacent pieces, and each one projected in front of the other to produce an overhanging canopy, which was repeated over the door. Above this canopy was a panel of chamfered rails that rose to the vault, projecting forwards as it approached the ceiling. Three other panels of this west wall had smaller niches, arranged asymmetrically, each with wooden tracery of distinctly Chinese appearance; there were three similar panels at the west end of the south wall.

The wavy line formed by the diaper appears in both two and three dimensions, in the painted wall pattern and the moulded plaster of the ceiling; it is even repeated in the metal grid of the umbrella stands. Where the Chinese Room is predominantly rectilinear, the Cloister Room is restless and unresolved; it is one of the most mysterious ever designed by Mackintosh, as moodily atmospheric as the rooms at the Willow Tea Rooms were light and airy. It is important in showing the fruits of Mackintosh's break with the more organic style of the early 1900s, and shows him able to reintroduce curves and pattern into his designs. It was his last major work in Glasgow before World War I; the themes and motifs used in it were taken up again at 78 Derngate in 1916.

Mackintosh was on the verge of perfecting a style that would allow him to repeat the triumph of the School of Art Library on a smaller scale. He had virtually arrived at a formula that would have allowed him to synthesise the successful elements of that design into a truly modern style. The Cloister Room is totally new, not depending on any historical precedents, and it shows that Mackintosh was prepared to progress from the apparently unsurpassable work in the Library, which was his greatest achievement only because he was not given the opportunity to match it or improve on it. As the Library was designed before he was forty, he cannot have intended it to be his final masterpiece. The Chinese Room and the Cloister Room show that the Library interior was the beginning of a new phase, which the west elevation of the School of Art confirms. In the two small commissions for Miss Cranston in 1911, Mackintosh returned almost to the position he was in during the late 1890s, when he began to develop the ideas that culminated in the design for The Hill House.

While his interior designs of 1907-11 became increasingly adventurous and accomplished, there was little development in his furniture. The boxy shapes of 1904 remained, and the later tea room furniture was simple in the extreme. Even if wavy patterns were allowed to soften the box-like effect of the designs, they were firmly contained within a severely rectilinear outline. The more expensive cabinets and chairs designed for The Hill House and Hous'hill found few successors after 1904, but this was probably more the result of a lack of commissions than of any definite change in approach. Indeed, in 1912, he designed one of the most elaborate and elegant tables of his career, but there was no furniture of the period from 1907 to 1911 that adequately reflected the new ideas evident in his architecture and interior design. Even at Ingram Street in 1911, he seems to have been restrained, perhaps by the need for economy or the particular requirements of tea room furniture, and it was not until he left Glasgow that equivalent changes in his furniture designs became apparent.

WORK FOR W. J. BASSETT-LOWKE & OTHERS, 1916-2°

Mackintosh seems to have left the firm of Honeyman, Keppie & Mackintosh in 1913, but he did not make a success of working on his own in Glasgow and, with no new commissions and little prospect of any in the near future, decided to take an extended holiday from the city in which he had created so much of his best work. In 1914, the Mackintoshes left Glasgow for Walberswick, on the Suffolk coast, close by the Newberys, who often spent holidays there sketching and painting. For about a year, Mackintosh spent his time painting watercolour studies of flowers, and he began to develop a new style of landscape painting in the hope of making a living as an artist. Newbery's daughter, Mary Newbery Sturrock, was in Walberswick in 1914 and believes that Mackintosh was about to leave for Vienna, but the start of World War I effectively prevented this.

Vienna might have offered no greater opportunities for new work, but it did have a thriving artistic community that would have provided Mackintosh with the moral support that he lacked in Glasgow. The furniture he produced in Northampton in 1916-19 also shows that his new ideas were extremely close to some of the developments in furniture design that had taken place in Vienna since his last recorded visit there in 1900. In the years after the appearance of his work at the Secession exhibition, many of the younger designers looked as much to him as they did to Hoffmann and Moser; if there was a Mackintosh School anywhere, it was as much in Vienna as in Glasgow.

At home, apart from the work of his friends James Salmon Jr and J. Gaff Gillespie, who were virtually the only Scottish architects to develop a new style based on the same principles as Mackintosh's work, his influence on furniture design appeared only in the diluted form of shop-commissioned designs by men like E.A. Taylor, George Logan and John Ednie. In Vienna, the young designers built on Mackintosh's ideas and gradually developed a style of their own. This was on the whole rather more lavish, using expensive and luxurious materials, with an emphasis on exquisite craftsmanship, which Mackintosh rarely demanded of his furniture-makers. Ironically, such men as Otto Prutscher, who had been one of Mackintosh's most ardent disciples, produced during the years 1907-10 much the same sort of designs as Mackintosh turned to in 1916-17. He was obviously aware of

Hall at 78 Derngate, Northampton. The photograph shows a Bassett-Lowke family party but is also the only illustration of the door screen (wood, lacquered black, with silk panels) fully extended; it was a draught screen, forming a corridor between the street door and the rest of the hall-parlour. From contemporary photographs and descriptions it appears to have been covered in purple material with an inverted triangle of yellow silk at the top of each of the four panels. Hall, 1916.D. Screen, untraced, 1916.12

Hall at 78 Derngate, Northampton. Hunterian Art Gallery, University of Glasgow. 1916.F.

Hall at 78 Derngate, Northampton. Looking towards the staircase screen (wood, painted black, with panels of leaded glass) with the door to the dining-room in the far corner. Mackintosh re-located the staircase across the middle of the house and hid both up and down flights behind this lattice screen. As the staircase climbs, the lattice is left open but the lower sections are filled with either flat panels of wood or decorative panels of coloured and leaded glass. Hall, Hunterian Art Gallery, University of Glasgow, 1916.E. Screen, *in situ*, 1916.4.

Dining room at 78 Derngate, Northampton. Hunterian Art Gallery, University of Glasgow. 1916.G.

Dining room at 78 Derngate, Northampton. This photograph shows the table lamp and standard lamp which are now both lost. Hunterian Art Gallery, University of Glasgow. 1916.H. Table lamp, 1916.33. Standard lamp, 1916.32.

The main bedroom at 78 Derngate, Northampton. Hunterian Art Gallery, University of Glasgow. 1916.I.

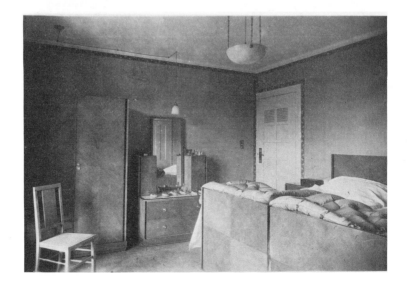

78 Derngate, Northampton. *Left:* Garden elevation. Hunterian Art Gallery, University of Glasgow. 1916.C. *Right:* Staircase from first to second floor. Hunterian Art Gallery, University of Glasgow. 1916.L. *Opposite page. Left:* Lamp standard and shade (standard, walnut; shade, silk on a metal frame). Although walnut was used extensively in the dining room this is the only use of it in the hall, where all the other pieces were painted black. The triangular motifs from the wall stencils are here repeated on the shade. Northampton Museum. 1916.5. *Right:* Fireplace for the hall (wood, painted black). The grate is wrought iron and very similar to several of the earlier grates. The wooden mantelpiece has a stepped, moulded pattern which has its antecedents in the west door of the Glasgow School of Art, designed in 1907. *In situ.* 1916.7.

Prutscher's work, although there are rarely any literal correspondences between his own designs and earlier ones by Prutscher, apart from the clock for the Derngate guest bedroom. The idea of any degree of plagiarism is banished by the way in which Mackintosh reacted to the Viennese work and the totally different approach he adopted to interior design and decoration during the war years. He had always been ready to absorb ideas from other sources, but was not a true eclectic. From 1905 onwards, the mainstream of his work gradually progressed towards the same conclusions that were reached by the Viennese around 1908-10. Unfortunately, Mackintosh had little opportunity to put the new ideas that appeared in his interiors into practice in his designs for furniture. From the illustrations of furniture by Prutscher and his colleagues, Mackintosh was able to extract what he needed to transform his own tentative experiments into the fully fledged new style of 1916-17. To Mackintosh, this would have been similar to the processes of extracting motifs from nature and from vernacular and medieval buildings. The result was pure Mackintosh, for his ideas, whatever their source, were not literally regurgitated but were absorbed into a new and coherent set of designs.

After about a year in Walberswick, Mackintosh and his wife moved to London, where they rented studios in Glebe Place, Chelsea. Mackintosh received a number of commissions from friends and neighbours in Chelsea for studios, a block of flats and even a theatre, but most of these proved abortive; none of the executed commissions appears to have contained any significant interiors or furniture. One client from outside London, however, provided Mackintosh with the opportunity to recapture the flair of his Glasgow work in a series of interiors for houses in and around Northampton.

W.J. Bassett-Lowke, a manufacturer of scale models and one of the early members of the Design & Industries Association, would have been aware of recent artistic developments in Austria and Germany and before 1914 had contacts with the Deutscher Werkbund. Above all, he was anxious to foster new standards and to commission designers who were new at least to him. Bassett-Lowke had not heard of Mackintosh before 1914, when, as he wrote in a series of notes dated 22nd August 1939, 'during a holiday in Cornwall I met a friend from Glasgow who held forth to me on the merits of the artist architect Chas Rennie Mackintosh.' His search for Mackintosh evidently took him to Glasgow, as Mrs Newbery Sturrock remembers him staying with or visiting the Newberys. This was after the outbreak of war, and Bassett-Lowke probably made contact with Mackintosh towards the end of 1915. The project he had in mind was the renovation of a small terraced house in the centre of Northampton, 78 Derngate, into which he intended to move after his forthcoming marriage in 1917. Mackintosh had already left Glasgow when Bassett-Lowke travelled north to find him, but the prospective client would undoubtedly have taken the opportunity to see for himself the work that Mackintosh had carried out there. Mackintosh was traced to London, and work on the new commission was probably started late in 1915 or early in 1916.

Although it was by no means as large a job as The Hill House or the renovations at Hous'hill, it offered a considerable challenge to Mackintosh, not only the personal one of whether he could again carry through such a commission, but also the challenge of working within such tight confines and of producing a design to manipulate the available space and impose complete aesthetic control over it. Bassett-Lowke proved a demanding client, perhaps Mackintosh's most knowledgeable in the field of design. He was certainly unlike the others in one major respect: his house, and later his country cottage, were to contain furniture designed by the client as well as by the architect; he was not afraid to make specific, as well as more sweeping criticisms of the proposals submitted to him, and it says much for Mackintosh that he was able to leave so strong a personal imprint on so small a job for such a demanding client.

In his awareness of developments in Europe and his openness to new ideas, Bassett-Lowke would have acted as a catalyst to Mackintosh and given him the opportunity to develop the theories he had begun to elaborate in Glasgow. How far Bassett-Lowke led Mackintosh to his new style and how far Mackintosh forced it upon him we shall never know. It is quite obvious, though, that Mackintosh made a greater change in his furniture style than he had ever attempted before. Where much of the Glasgow work can be seen as a steady progression, there is an enormous gulf between the furniture of 1910-11 and that designed for the Northampton jobs. Ideas tentatively expressed at Ingram Street appeared as a mature style at 78 Derngate, yet there was no intervening work in which Mackintosh was able to develop his Glasgow designs. Two years' rest and the enthusiasm of Bassett-Lowke seem to have been sufficient to produce these radical changes.

As an engineering model-maker, Bassett Lowke was conscious of new developments in technology and keenly interested in efficiency in all things, but particularly in design. Just as strict economy was an important factor in the modernity of Mackintosh's austere designs for the Glasgow School of Art, so Bassett-Lowke's insistence on clean lines, unfussy decoration and solid construction would have speeded Mackintosh's reaction to the Viennese work of 1908-10.

There is another major difference between this commission and much of the Glasgow work: while in his native city, Mackintosh would have stood over his furniture-maker, amending the design as work progressed; once he

78 Derngate, Northampton. *Opposite page.* *Top left:* Smoker's cabinet (wood, lacquered black, with plastic inlay). Mackintosh had used a synthetic material based on casein in the Chinese Room in Glasgow but this is the first occurrence of his using it (Erinoid) in a piece of furniture, here in the inlaid diamonds and triangles. Victoria and Albert Museum, London. 1916.16. *Centre left:* Cabinet for the hall (wood, lacquered black). The lattice theme was repeated here on a smaller scale but the mirrors, by reflecting the rest of the hall, made this tiny room seem that much larger. Victoria and Albert Museum, London. 1916.9. *Top right:* Dressing table and mirror for the main bedroom (sycamore, stained grey and polished, with

black inlay). Another severe and simple piece, relying for effect on the pattern of the grain of the timber on drawers and cupboards. The black inlay was only used to emphasise the outer edges of the piece and not horizontally or in such profusion as the linear stencilling on the guest bedroom furniture of 1919. Untraced. 1916.35.
Bottom right: Chair for the hall (wood, lacquered black). The top rail and front apron rail are decorated with incised lines to produce a pattern reminiscent of some of the decorative woodwork in the Chinese Room in Glasgow. Victoria and Albert Museum, London. 1916.11.

197

left, he had to rely upon his drawings to convey his requirements to the craftsmen. And Bassett-Lowke did use craftsmen. Many items were made by German immigrant workers, probably with experience of Werkbund methods and materials; others were made by local or London cabinet-makers (probably Heals, who made the carpets at 78 Derngate) or by Bassett-Lowke's own employees in his factory. Accordingly, the Northampton furniture is better made than any of the Glasgow pieces, although this is partly due to the design, which took more account than was usual for Mackintosh of the suitability of materials. These rather plain pieces, with little emphasis on complicated curves and awkward changes of section, provided enough timber to allow strong, traditional methods of construction. Indeed, many of these pieces, with their clean lines and simple applied decoration, would have been ideal for mass production.

With the exception of the more expressionist pieces for the hall, much of the furniture designed for 78 Derngate relies for its effect on its mass, on severe outlines and plain surfaces. Decoration is achieved by manipulating the grain of the timber, transposing it in adjacent doors of wardrobes and drawers of dressing tables, by piercing square holes through the panels of beds and cabinets, by introducing lattice-work gables, or by inlaying pieces of mother-of-pearl or occasionally a synthetic material, usually Erinoid. Timber – oak, mahogany or sycamore – is chosen for its grain and rarely stained but simply waxed and polished. In the main bedroom, and in the later suite for the guest bedroom of 1919, a simple stencilled strip is applied to the edges of the pieces; in the 1919 furniture, this was also used on the divisions between drawers and even the junctions between the panels of the bedheads and footboards. Only in the hall furniture is the wood stained black to match the wall decorations. This furniture is altogether more expressive: curves combine with lattice patterns on the chairs and settle, and the fireplace adopts the style of moulded architrave used in the door in the west elevation of the School of Art. No organic motifs are to be seen in the decoration. Even the hall stencils make a break with all Mackintosh's earlier stencilling except that in the Cloister Room of 1911. The emphasis is entirely on geometrical forms – squares, triangles, oblongs and, rarely, circles.

The Derngate designs are as much furniture for the second machine age as anything by Mies van der Rohe, Marcel Breuer or Le Corbusier, but they rely on traditional materials. Like the Library at the School of Art, they are modern without being rebellious. Mackintosh did not feel the need to use chrome, steel, leather or plate glass to make new statements. In a curious way, at the same time that the International Style has come under attack by contemporary architects, the new generation of furniture designers has returned to timber and more traditional materials, often producing furniture that is quite close to many of the Derngate pieces. Even so, Mackintosh's Northampton designs, unlike his furniture of 1897-1907, are virtually unknown. What is now recognised in young designers' work as a good, straightforward approach to the problems of designing in a modern idiom with traditional materials had been accomplished by Mackintosh almost seventy years ago.

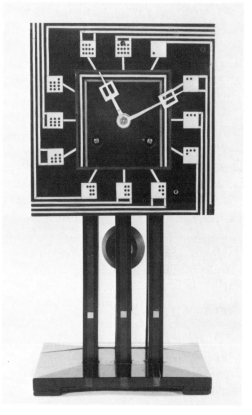

Above: Settle for the hall, 78 Derngate, Northampton (wood, lacquered black). Designed to match the hall chairs, with the same emphasis on a lattice motif and incised top and apron rails. Victoria and Albert Museum. 1916.13. *Left:* Clock with ten columns for 78 Derngate, Northampton (ebonised wood, inlaid with ivory and green Erinoid). A development of the clock designed for The Hill House in 1905. The contrast between the blackness of the wood and the colours of the ivory and the Erinoid, however, has a much more dramatic effect. This clock, and the others designed in 1917, look forward to the Art Deco style of the 1920s. Richmond Museum, Virginia (Sidney and Frances Lewis Collection). 1917.7. *Right:* Clock with six columns and domino figures for W.J. Bassett-Lowke (ebonised wood, inlaid with ivory and green and purple Erinoid). A more abstract or modern approach to clock design than the clock with ten columns. 1917.4.

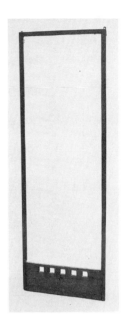

78 Derngate, Northampton. *Top left:* Barometer (ebonised wood and mother-of-pearl). Designed to fit into one of the panels in the staircase screen in the hall. 1917.9. *Top centre:* Candlestick (possibly Erinoid). The only item known to have been designed by Mackintosh and made entirely from a synthetic material, rather than from sheet material. British Museum, London. 1917.8. *Top right:* Hanging mirror for the guest bedroom (mahogany). 1917.19. *Centre left:* Dressing table for the guest bedroom (mahogany, with ebonised wooden base and inlaid with mother-of-pearl and aluminium). Victoria and Albert Museum, London. 1917.11. *Bottom left:* Luggage stool for the guest bedroom (mahogany, with ebonised wooden feet). Victoria and Albert Museum, London. 1917.17. *Opposite page. Bottom left:* Wardrobe for the guest bedroom (mahogany, with ebonised wooden base and inlaid with mother-of-pearl). This first design for the guest bedroom furniture (it was replaced by a new design in 1919) was similar in style to the furniture in the main bedroom designed in 1916. It depends for its decorative effect on the broad massing of the planes of the timber, contrasting the lie of the grain where necessary, and offset by small panels of mother-of-pearl or aluminium. A second complete set of furniture was made for Bassett-Lowke's friend and business colleague, Sidney Horstmann, for his house in Bath; a third set, with minor variations, was made for another business associate, W. Franklin. The Derngate and Franklin furniture are in a private collection and the Horstmann pieces are in the Victoria and Albert Museum. Victoria and Albert Museum, London. 1917.10.

Top left: Ladderback armchair for the guest bedroom, 78 Derngate, Northampton (mahogany, with upholstered seat). Victoria and Albert Museum, London. 1917.12. *Top right:* Ladderback chair for the guest bedroom, 78 Derngate, Northampton (mahogany, with upholstered seat). Victoria and Albert Museum, London. 1917.13. *Bottom right:* Wardrobe for W. Franklin (mahogany, with ebonised wooden base and inlaid with mother-of-pearl). A variant of the Derngate wardrobe, having three sections instead of two. 1917.10A.

with ebonised wooden base and inlaid with mother-of-pearl). 1917.16. *Right:* Washstand for the guest bedroom (mahogany, with ebonised wooden base, inlaid with mother-of-pearl and aluminium, and with a printed fabric behind the glazed splashback). Although the washstands would originally have used a fabric designed by Mackintosh in the back panels, none of the original fabrics has survived. 1917.18. *Opposite page. Left:* Towel rail for the guest bedroom (mahogany). 1917.15. *Right:* Dressing table stool for the guest bedroom, 78 Derngate, Northampton (mahogany, with ebonised wooden feet and an upholstered seat). London. 1917.20. All Victoria and Albert Museum.

78 Derngate, Northampton. *Left:* Bedside cupboard for the guest bedroom (mahogany,

The house at 78 Derngate was brick-built with three floors facing the street and, because of the steeply sloping site, a lower floor at garden level. A photograph survives of the house before conversion on which are pencilled Mackintosh's intentions. These were the addition of a bay window about two metres wide, the insertion of a small window for the lavatory in the existing blind recess, a new window of the same size as the existing one for the first floor bathroom, and a new front door and deadlight, although the existing architraves were not altered. At the back of the house, the alterations were more spectacular; as Thomas Howarth has pointed out, the finished elevation predates any other Modern Movement work in Britain. An extension was built to almost the full width of the house, about 1.3 metres deep and three storeys high, providing the top-floor bedroom (the third floor on this elevation) with an open balcony, the main bedroom

with an enclosed balcony and the dining room and basement kitchen with much-needed extra space. This extension and the whole rear wall of the house were finished in white cement; with its sharp angles, broad openings and sun blinds, it seems prophetic of the International Style.

Internally, the main change was the relocation of the staircase. Originally, the front door opened into a narrow hall with the staircase on the left, severely restricting the size of the parlour. Mackintosh placed a new staircase parallel to the dividing wall between the front and back rooms, increasing the size of the hall. The front door then opened straight into the new hall-parlour, which Mackintosh had originally intended to screen with a curtain. In a letter dated 31st July 1916 (the day he gained possesssion of the house), Bassett-Lowke suggested that the door be rehinged to open flat against the wall and that a folding screen should be substituted for the curtain. Mack-intosh seems to have concurred readily, but the screen cannot now be traced. The new front door was painted black and had panels of leaded glass with a triangular motif; above it, the deadlight was surrounded by a miniature version of the stepped architrave of the door in the west elevation of the Glasgow School of Art.

The black paint and triangles of the front door were the keynote of the new hall. All the furniture was black, as were the walls, which were relieved only by a chequered band of black and white squares. Above this band, forming a frieze around the room, was a stencilled pattern of overlaid triangles in yellow, grey, vermilion, blue, emerald green and purple. Even the ceiling was black, and the carpet had a pattern of black and grey. The triangle motif also appeared in panels of leaded glass placed at random on the lattice screen that masked the flights of stairs up to the bedrooms and down to the kitchen; other panels of the screen were open or solid wood, a treatment that Mackintosh had used in the Chinese Room at Ingram Street in 1911, and earlier in the exhibition stand for Wilkinson, Heywood & Clark in 1906. The hall furniture was also based on the square lattice, ex-cept for the smoking cabinet and the door screen, which were decorated with triangles. The fireplace had a simple wrought iron grate surrounded by cement render and a black wooden mantel with a stepped outline that again echoed the west front of the School of Art.

Beyond the hall on the ground floor was the dining room, for which Bassett-Lowke seems to have designed much of the movable furniture including the tables, chairs and sideboard, and a curious circular tea table with an inlaid top. Mackintosh's contributions appear to have been the decorations, the fittings, a standard lamp and a table lamp. Beneath the wide picture rail, the walls were divided into panels by means of walnut straps, between which Mackintosh used a dark wallpaper with a leaf and berry motif, probably his only use of patterned wallpaper as opposed to stencilling (although he may have used a similar paper in the first guest bedroom of 1917). The ceiling and frieze were white. On either side of the fireplace were fitted cupboards, the upper sections glazed for crockery, the lower with drawers, shelves and pivoted boxes for wood and coal. The surround to the grate was of white tiles, with oblong blue tiles introduced for pattern. All the woodwork was matt-finished walnut. Over the fireplace was a large mirror, at each end of which was a lantern. Thomas Howarth has suggested a source for these in Josef Urban's work in Vienna, which had been illustrated in an article, 'The Art Revival in Austria', in a 1906 special number of *The Studio*.

The main bedroom and bathroom occupied the first floor, with French windows in the bedroom giving access to a covered verandah that was open on the south and west, looking over the garden. The bedroom had white enamelled woodwork and was wallpapered in grey, without a picture rail, but with a narrow mauve figured edging. Mackintosh designed the furniture in grey sycamore, making extensive use of quartered panels, turning the direction of the grain to produce a pattern. A black inlay, about 2 cm. wide, was used along the vertical edges of all the pieces, defining the outer dimensions of what is otherwise a very bland design. There is no record of the number of items designed for this bedroom; the surviving photograph shows twin beds, bedside tables, a dressing table and a wardrobe, as well as a chair that was probably not designed by Mackintosh. A washstand was not required, as the room had a fitted basin; the only other likely item would have been a dressing mirror, of which there is no trace, but then none of the furniture for this bedroom seems to have survived.

The staircase between the first and second floors continued the lattice theme, but with white paint; all the square panels were open to admit light, except those at the ends of the stair treads. The cupboard doors, and the bathroom wall and door all repeated the lattice motif, the upper two rows on the bathroom wall being glazed to provide borrowed light for the stairwell.

On the top floor was the guest bedroom, which did not originally have the furniture and decorations that are preserved in the Hunterian Art Gallery and date from 1919. According to Mrs Cutting, a niece of Mrs W.J. Bassett-Lowke, the guest bedroom was originally furnished in mahogany inlaid with mother-of-pearl. This suite was probably sold in 1919 or 1920 to a local furniture dealer, Mr Cave, who left it to his daughter (also a dealer), who in turn sold it without recording the name of the new owner.

Stylistically, the mahogany furniture has much in common with the main bedroom designs. It relies for its effect on broad, unmodelled planes of timber relieved by mother-of-pearl or aluminium inlay rather than the black edging that was applied to the sycamore pieces. This mahogany furniture is also very similar in mass and outline to that of the main bedroom. The decorations of the guest bedroom also appear to have been similar: Mackintosh's drawing for the room shows a figured wallpaper with stencilled vertical borders in the corners of the room.

No photographs of the original guest bedroom survive, but the furniture was probably laid out in a similar way to that adopted in 1919, as is confirmed by photographs of an identical suite for Bassett-Lowke's friend, Sidney Horstmann. This furniture, made for Horstmann's house in Bath, has survived complete and is now in the Victoria & Albert Museum; at least one drawing for the decoration of this bedroom and three contemporary photographs of it also exist. The Horstmann furniture was reputedly made by German craftsmen interned as enemy aliens on the Isle of Man, and the Derngate furniture probably came from the same source. The drawing for the Derngate guest bedroom suggests that it was not designed until some months after the Bassett-Lowkes moved into the house in the spring of 1917.

All the decorations for the room were obliterated by the new scheme in 1919, but it is possible that the Horstmann bedroom decorations (which

Work for Sidney Horstmann, Bath.
Left: Bedroom. The original Mackintosh fabric used on the washstand can be clearly seen in this contemporary photograph. Victoria and Albert Museum, London. 1917.A.

Top right: Bedroom – detail of the Mackintosh fabric behind the beds. Victoria and Albert Museum, London. 1917.C.

Bottom right: Bedroom – the fireplace wall. Victoria and Albert Museum, London. 1917.B.

have also been overpainted) repeated those at Derngate. For the Horstmann bedroom, Mackintosh created a pattern out of stencilled strips, each approximately 5 cm. wide; some are of solid colour and others are composed of small triangles of different hues. They seem to have been run around the room at frieze level, with variations around the doors. A solid strip ran above the skirting board and was diverted around fixtures such as the fireplace, door and beds. Behind the beds was a panel of fabric designed by Mackintosh and also used for the curtains and the splash-back of the washstand. Even if this decorative scheme was not used at Derngate, it may well have inspired Bassett-Lowke's request for the 1919 alterations there. Certainly several of the features, like the panel behind the bed and the strips, foreshadow the 1919 scheme at Derngate. The Horstmann decorations do not appear to have been particularly successful, and Mackintosh may well have learned from them when he came to redesign the guest bedroom for Bassett-Lowke.

Nikolaus Pevsner considered Mackintosh's work at Derngate mannered, a criticism that surely cannot be justified. Mackintosh seems to have wanted to break with his Glasgow style, even with that of the School of Art Library or the Chinese Room, and this was his first opportunity in much the same way as *Anemones* and *Begonias* were to be the first stages in his new career as a watercolourist. Derngate anticipated European work of the next decade; it surpassed most of the designs of the 1920s and equalled the best of them, but, sadly, there was little to follow it.

Mackintosh's later work is often considered heavy and uncharacteristic of him. In fact, he was returning to some of the ideas he first developed at Argyle Street: broad planes and natural timber, but with the heaviness replaced by careful deployment of geometrical motifs to emphasise the simple shapes of the furniture and, on occasion, to give it a bold, sharp impact. The interiors at Derngate should not be regarded as the culmination of a fine career, but as the beginning of a new, albeit abortive one.

Mackintosh's last work in Glasgow was in 1917 for Miss Cranston, a new room at the Willow Tea Rooms, for which she chose a wartime theme, calling it The Dug-Out. By 1977, virtually all traces of it had disappeared, which is particularly sad as it represented an important development of the new style seen in the hall at Derngate. No photographs were taken of the finished interiors, and only a few drawings, a dozen pieces of furniture and two large paintings remain to give an indication of the design. The site was in the basement of the shop to the west of the Willow Tea Rooms. Mackintosh removed the fireplace from the front saloon and created a new stair down to the adjacent basement.

Mackintosh turned the absence of daylight in the basement to his advantage by creating a dramatic interior with shiny black ceilings and dark walls highlighted by patches of strong colour in the decorations and by the artificial lighting. A centrepiece in the back room was the Memorial Fireplace, which was decorated with inlaid glass and paintings of the flags of the opposing nations; above this commemorative plaque was a panel of decoration (probably stencilled) in the form of chequers, diamonds and triangles, all in the bright colours first used in the Derngate frieze. The back room possibly

The Dug Out, Willow Tea Rooms, Glasgow. *Top left:* Settle (painted wood), variant of that designed for 78 Derngate in 1916. Glasgow School of Art. 1917.30. *Bottom left:* Tea table (wood, stained dark). Glasgow School of Art. 1917.32. *Right:* Chair (painted wood). 1917.31.

also housed the two large paintings, *The Little Hills*. They were supposedly inspired by the words of the 65th Psalm, 'Thou crownest the year with Thy goodness . . . and the little hills shall rejoice,' and Mrs Sturrock remembers Margaret at work on them while the Mackintoshes were in Walberswick, which they had left by midsummer 1915. The paintings, then, were probably not conceived as decorations for The Dug-Out, and it is likely that they were shown at the Arts & Crafts Society in 1916, as part of a series entitled *Voices of the Woods*. Mackintosh may well have been involved in their design, even if Margaret was responsible for their execution – certainly they show a controlled strength that would have been thoroughly untypical of Margaret.

Two elevations of walls in The Dug-Out indicate the rooms' general appearance. Features from Derngate have been liberally translated to Glasgow, and without Bassett-Lowke looking critically over his shoulder, Mackintosh has been able to develop some of the ideas introduced in North-ampton. Whether or not these two drawings correspond with the completed

The Dug-Out, Willow Tea Rooms, Glasgow.
Top left: Table with cube and bobbin legs
(painted wood). Glasgow School of Art.
1917.33. *Bottom left:* Circular table with bobbin
legs (painted wood). Mackintosh incorporated
several traditional cabinet-maker's motifs in
The Dug-Out furniture but none is as decidedly
conventional as this table. Untraced. 1917.34.
Right: Ladderback armchair (painted wood).
Mackintosh designed similar ladderbacks for
the guest bedroom at 78 Derngate in 1917.
Glasgow School of Art. 1917.35.

work, one can see that strong linear patterns and dark colours relieved by
small patches of red, blue and green were to dominate the decorations. The
triangle appears in a less obvious role (around the door to the ladies' lavatory), but the square lattice is as prominent as ever. The furniture shown in
these designs seems simpler and less elegant than that for Derngate, partly
because Mackintosh has used a square stick of timber with a cross-section
larger than is usual in his furniture. This gives the chairs in particular a
heavier, slightly ungainly, appearance, which was almost certainly necessary to make them stand out against the decorations. At Derngate, the
decorations were successful because of their sustained impact in small rooms;
had the decorations of The Dug-Out survived, it would have been interesting to see how Mackintosh tackled the problems of using the same decorative
style on a larger scale.

Mackintosh's next work for Bassett-Lowke was in Candida Cottage at
Roade, near Northampton, and was restricted to the design of the dining

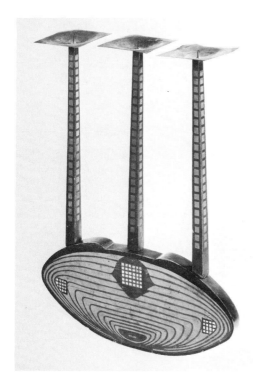

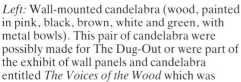

Left: Wall-mounted candelabra (wood, painted in pink, black, brown, white and green, with metal bowls). This pair of candelabra were possibly made for The Dug-Out or were part of the exhibit of wall panels and candelabra entitled *The Voices of the Wood* which was

shown at the 11th Exhibition of the Arts & Crafts Exhibition Society in 1916. 1917.37.
Right: Large ladderback armchair for The Dug-Out, Willow Tea Rooms, Glasgow (painted wood). Glasgow School of Art. 1917.36.

room furniture and decorations. Here he reverted to his customary pattern of a white ceiling and dark brown paper for the walls, which were decorated with a stencil pattern: a line of dark, square 'dots' and paler, long 'dashes' encircled the room just below the ceiling; at re-entrant corners and by the door, Mackintosh introduced a stencilled vertical ladder of blue rungs interrupted near the top by an abstract pattern of black and red linear shapes. The rungs were formed by three different stencils which could be reversed or inverted to create nine variations, and no two ladders appear to have been assembled in exactly the same way.

The furniture is probably the most modern and utilitarian that Mackintosh ever designed. Not only has the carved organic decoration of the early Glasgow period gone, but so has much of the lattice work and the geometricality of the later Glasgow and Derngate designs. Shapes are simple and robust, the decoration is quiet and the materials are basic: stained oak and the new materials Erinoid and Rexine. This is, perhaps, the closest Mackintosh ever came to the furniture of such English designers as Ernest Gimson or the Barnsleys; it anticipated the best 'thirties work of R.D. Russell and others, looking forward almost to the Utility designs produced during and after World War II.

The following year, Mackintosh was asked to repeat the dining room design for Bassett-Lowke's brother-in-law, F. Jones. This appears to be the

Candida Cottage, Roade, Northamptonshire.
Opposite page. Above: Dining room. Hunterian
Art Gallery, University of Glasgow.
1918.A. *Top left:* Sideboard for W. Franklin
(mahogany, inlaid with mother-of-pearl and
aluminium). Mackintosh gave Bassett-Lowke
two alternative designs for his Candida Cottage
sideboard; this is the option that Bassett-Lowke
rejected. 1918.2A. *Bottom left:* Coffee table
(oak, stained and waxed, inlaid with Radolith).
Brighton Museum and Art Gallery. 1918.3.
Top right: Service trolley (oak, stained and
waxed, inlaid with Radolith). Brighton
Museum and Art Gallery. 1918.4. *Bottom
right:* Dining table (oak, stained and waxed,
inlaid with Radolith). Brighton Museum and
Art Gallery. 1918.5. *This page. Above:* Dining
room. Hunterian Art Gallery, University of
Glasgow. 1918.B. *Right:* Dining chair (oak,
stained and waxed, inlaid with Radolith and
upholstered with Rexine). Brighton Museum
and Art Gallery. 1918.6.

only work he did at Jones's house in The Drive, Northampton. The treatment of the walls and ceiling was the same as at Candida Cottage, except
that the ladder stencil was repeated in the middle of the wall on either side
of two bracket lamps fitted over the sideboard. These were semicircular in
plan and very close to the design originally proposed for the Derngate
dining room.

Left: Dining room at The Drive, Northampton, for F. Jones. A repetition of the Candida Cottage design. Hunterian Art Gallery, University of Glasgow. 1919.A. *Right:* Guest bedroom, 78 Derngate, Northampton. This contemporary photograph shows the arrangement of the furniture within the room and the way in which the striped panel behind the beds was carried on to the ceiling. Hunterian Art Gallery, University of Glasgow. 1919.B.

Late in 1919, Mackintosh was recalled to Derngate to redesign both the furniture and the decorations for the guest bedroom. The result was very striking, and Bassett-Lowke's notes describe it as 'perhaps the most daring in the house'. The wall behind the twin beds was covered with black and white striped paper extending the width of the beds and their shared bedside table. Mackintosh had used this paper before on the attic staircase of 78 Southpark Avenue, but here he carried it up on to the ceiling, where it extended the length of the beds. The outer stripes turned through an angle of 90°, mitred like a picture frame to form the end of the ceiling panel. The perimeter stripe was a piece of ultramarine blue ribbon, which was also used above the bedside table and at the edges of the wall panel, where it was held in place by black-headed tacks. On the ceiling, two striped panels, each about 60 cm. wide, projected from the outer edges of the main panel; these continued down the walls and were again turned through 90° towards each other to meet over the window, forming another lattice pattern. The curtains matched the paper, with lattice-work at the bottom and *appliqué* squares of blue silk edged with emerald green. The bedspreads followed a similar arrangement.

One would have expected the furniture to be overpowered by such a bold decorative scheme, especially in a room roughly four metres square. However, Mackintosh's designs for the furniture were simple and severe; the rather austere shapes in light oak with a narrow edging of blue squares on a black strip stood up admirably to the exciting decorations. The motif of the square was dominant again, where in the more restrained main bedroom decoration was almost non-existent.

Mackintosh designed over a dozen pieces of furniture for this room. The surviving wide-angle photographs of them *in situ* distort their scale, and every item is actually smaller than it appears in the photographs. In its context, the furniture does not seem undersized; in isolation, the pieces can

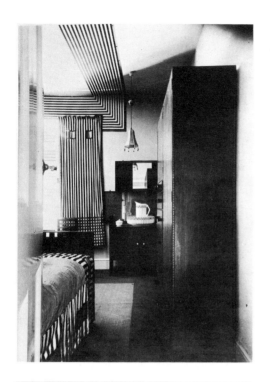

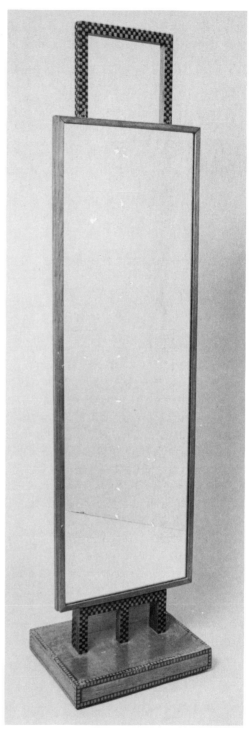

78 Derngate, Northampton. *Top left:* Guest bedroom. The striped pattern on the ceiling was returned on the window wall and the curtains were made of a matching material. Hunterian Art Gallery, University of Glasgow. 1919.C. *Bottom left:* Gentleman's bedside table for the guest bedroom (oak, with ebonised base and handles). A companion piece to the dressing table, for the use of male guests, with drawers for collars and cuff-links etc. 1919.5. *Right:* Cheval mirror for the guest bedroom (oak, with blue-and-black chequer decoration). Hunterian Art Gallery, University of Glasgow. 1919.8.

78 Derngate, Northampton. *Top left:* Luggage stool for the guest bedroom (oak, with blue-and-black chequer decoration). Hunterian Art Gallery, University of Glasgow. 1919.9. *Centre left:* Dressing table stool for the guest bedroom (oak). Hunterian Art Gallery, University of Glasgow. 1919.11. *Bottom left:* Dressing table and washstand for the guest bedroom, 78 Derngate, Northampton (oak, with blue-and-

black chequer decoration). Hunterian Art Gallery, University of Glasgow. 1919.10. *Opposite page. Top right:* Chair for guest bedroom (oak, with blue-and-black chequer decoration). Hunterian Art Gallery, University of Glasgow. 1919.4. *Bottom right:* Clock for the guest bedroom (oak, with black stencilled decoration and mother-of-pearl face). The largest of the clocks designed by Mackintosh for

Bassett-Lowke. The design is almost certainly based on a clock by Otto Prutscher, a Viennese designer. British Museum, London. 1919.7. *This page. Left:* Bedside cabinet for the guest bedroom (oak, with ebonised handles). Hunterian Art Gallery, University of Glasgow. 1919.2. *Right:* Wardrobe for the guest bedroom (oak, with blue-and-black chequer decoration, with an ebonised base and inlaid with mother-of-pearl). Hunterian Art Gallery, University of Glasgow. 1919.6.

look somewhat disturbing. In the room, which is now displayed at the Hunterian Art Gallery in Glasgow, Mackintosh prevents a feeling of claustrophobia by using large areas of unmodelled timber. It was the last interior of any consequence that he produced – a striking note on which to end a brilliant career.

Mackintosh was recalled to Derngate for the last time in 1920 to make alterations to the decoration of the hall. The effect of the black walls with a frieze of brilliantly coloured triangles would have been largely lost on Bassett-Lowke, who is believed to have been colour blind. In any case, by 1920, his wife, at least, was beginning to find the energetic composition rather wearing – his friends had apparently always considered the hall a little extreme.

Accordingly, the woodwork was painted grey and Mackintosh devised a new frieze based on the same general principles as the earlier design, but smaller in scale and not so deep. Bassett-Lowke obviously approved of it, as he used it again in his study at New Ways. His notes on Derngate indicate that he had hoped to commission this new house from Mackintosh, but the architect had left London for the south of France. Bassett-Lowke

was unable to make contact with him, and New Ways was designed by Peter Behrens.

Mackintosh's last furniture had been designed when he was only 52. There were no other commissions in view, nor were there any for buildings or interiors. In 1923, Mackintosh gave up any faint hope he may still have had of making a new career in London and went to the south of France to paint watercolours, living in genteel poverty on what was left of his savings and on Margaret's small private income. What he had achieved since leaving Glasgow was virtually unknown outside a small circle of friends, and even the three extensive articles on his work for Bassett-Lowke in Northampton never mentioned his name. He was possibly less bitter than he had been at his failure to overcome the 'Enemy' in Glasgow, where he

Left: The hall at 78 Derngate, Northampton. 1920.B. *Right:* The hall at 78 Derngate, Northampton. After World War II Bassett-Lowke was prevailed upon by his wife to replace the predominantly black colour scheme of the hall with something less crepuscular. Mackintosh prepared a design in pale grey incorporating a new frieze of stencils. This photograph, taken by Bassett-Lowke, shows the hall before the stencils were finished. Hunterian Art Gallery, University of Glasgow. 1920.A. *Below:* The study at New Ways,

Northampton. In 1923 Bassett-Lowke decided to leave Derngate but discovered that Mackintosh had left the country and was no longer practising as an architect. Instead he turned to Peter Behrens for a design for his new house but he insisted on incorporating it in all of the furniture designed by Mackintosh for Derngate and the 1920 stencilled frieze for the hall. Hunterian Art Gallery University of Glasgow. 1925.A.

had fought for twenty years. All the same, his defeat was a grave disappointment for him and a tragic loss for British architecture and design.

In the 1920s and 1930s, Mackintosh, like so many of the designers and architects from the two decades before World War I, was forgotten and his work neglected, passed over by the frivolous practitioners of Art Deco. Even Bauhaus-trained students were, not unnaturally, looking up to Mies van der Rohe and to Walter Gropius, and they ignored the designers of the earlier generation whose work had provided the antecedents for the Bauhaus and all it stood for. In the late 1930s, and with some detachment, Nikolaus Pevsner recognised Mackintosh's contribution and extracted him from the mire into which everyone connected with Art Nouveau had been thrown. Certainly, whatever else Mackintosh was, he was no Art Nouveau designer. He and Margaret both disliked the wild gyrations of the florid French and Belgian furniture and metalwork, but too often their work was linked with it and their reputations suffered as a consequence. One can see how perhaps the Room de Luxe at the Willow Tea Rooms might at first glance seem to fall under the umbrella of Art Nouveau, but Mackintosh's work as a whole stands outside the mainstream of his period.

Other architects believed, as Mackintosh did, in the total environment, embracing the design of all the individual components in a room or even a whole building. Josef Hoffmann, C.F.A. Voysey and M.H. Baillie Scott achieved it, but in a manner totally different from that adopted by Mackintosh. While much of Hoffmann's furniture, for instance, works well in the spaces for which it was designed, it often loses impact or appeal when removed from its intended setting. On the other hand, Baillie Scott's furniture, seen out of context, can be pedestrian – well made and handsome, but all too often dull. Voysey's furniture is repetitive, based on his well-tried combinations of structure and decorative motif – worthy, perhaps, but unexciting.

Mackintosh's furniture is exciting in its approach to the problems of design and of the manipulation of mass and space, line and colour. His approach is that of an artist: while form may follow function, it is never automatically reduced to an ergonomic formula. Each piece of furniture is conceived as a separate work of art. Mackintosh's genius lay not just in his ability to create such forms, but in the skill with which he could bring them together in harmony with the spatial compositions of his buildings. Whether working within the confines of traditional technology or exploring its outer limits, he applied the same principles. His furniture was conceived as sculpture. For Mackintosh, beauty lay in art, not in mindless utility, and he exhorted his fellow artists, architects and craftsmen to work for the same ideals. He preached individuality where others searched for uniformity and all too often found it in mediocrity. He sought a new vocabulary untainted by historicism and yet at the same time aware of precedent. Achieving this, he acted, in the words of Mies van der Rohe, as 'a purifier in the field of architecture'.

BIBLIOGRAPHY

Filippo Alison, *Charles Rennie Mackintosh as a Designer of Chairs*, London, 1974, the English language edition, trans. Bruno and Christina del Priore, of Alison's catalogue to the Milan exhibition, *Le Sedie di Charles Rennie Mackintosh*, 1973; with photographs of original drawings and of reproductions of some of Mackintosh's chairs.

Roger Billcliffe, *Charles Rennie Mackintosh: The Complete Furniture, Furniture Drawings and Interior Designs*, Guildford, 1979; second edition, 1980.

Roger Billcliffe, *Mackintosh Textile Designs*, London, 1982.

Roger Billcliffe and Peter Vergo, 'Charles Rennie Mackintosh and the Austrian Art Revival', *Burlington Magazine*, CXIX, 1977, pp. 739-46.

Elizabeth Bird, 'Ghouls and gaspipes: Public reaction to the early work of The Four', *Scottish Art Review* XIV.

Douglas Percy Bliss, *Charles Rennie Mackintosh and the Glasgow School of Art*, Glasgow, 1961.

Charles Rennie Mackintosh, an exhibition catalogue, Saltire Society and Arts Council of Great Britain, 1953.

Charles Rennie Mackintosh, 1868-1928: a memorial tribute, catalogue of an exhibition of Mackintosh material in the collection of Dr Thomas Howarth, The Art Gallery of Ontario, Toronto, 1978.

Jackie Cooper (ed), *Mackintosh Architecture*, with an introduction by Barbara Bernard, London, 1978.

Glasgow School of Art, *Some Examples of Furniture by Charles Rennie Mackintosh in the Glasgow School of Art Collection*, introduction by H. Jefferson Barnes, Glasgow, 1968.

Glasgow School of Art, *Some Examples of Metalwork by Charles Rennie Mackintosh at Glasgow School of Art*, introduction by H. Jefferson Barnes, Glasgow, 1968.

The Glasgow Style, catalogue of an exhibition at Glasgow Art Gallery, 1984.

Thomas Howarth, *Charles Rennie Mackintosh and the Modern Movement*, second edition, London, 1977. This is a facsimile reprint of the 1952 first edition supplemented by an enlarged bibliography and a new introduction.

Horst-Herbert Kossatz, 'The Vienna Secession and its Early Relations with Great Britain', *Studio International*, January 1971.

Gerald and Celia Larner, *The Glasgow Style*, Edinburgh, 1979.

Robert Macleod, *Charles Rennie Mackintosh*, Feltham, 1968; second edition, Glasgow, 1983.

Andrew McLaren Young, *Charles Rennie Mackintosh: Architecture, Design and Painting*, catalogue of an exhibition sponsored by the Edinburgh Festival Society and arranged by the Scottish Arts Council, 1968.

Margaret Macdonald Mackintosh, catalogue of an exhibition at the Hunterian Art Gallery, Glasgow, 1983.

Hermann Muthesius, *Das Englische Haus*, Berlin, 1904-05, 3 vols. Translation edited by Dennis Sharp, London, 1979.

Nikolaus Pevsner, 'Charles Rennie Mackintosh' in *Studies in Art, Architecture and Design*, Vol. II, London, 1968. This is a translation by Adeline Hartcup of Pevsner's pioneering study first published by Il Balcone, Milan, 1950.

Eduard Sekler, 'Mackintosh and Vienna' in *The Architectural Review*, CXLIV, 1968, pp. 455-56; reprinted and enlarged as the introduction to the Viennese catalogue of the 1968 Edinburgh Festival Mackintosh Exhibition.

Isobel Spencer, 'Francis Newbery and the Glasgow Style', *Apollo*, pp.286-93, 1973.

The Studio Special Number, *Modern British Domestic Architecture and Decoration*, London, 1901.

Peter Vergo, *Art in Vienna, 1898-1918*, London, 1975.

INDEX

Page numbers in italic refer to picture captions.

Ann Street, Glasgow. *See* Southpark Avenue
Argyle Street Tea Rooms, Glasgow 23, 27, 28, *28*, *29*, 30, *30*, 31, *32*, 88
—The Dutch Kitchen 160, 161, *162*
Art Deco 218
Art Nouveau 17, 218
Arts & Crafts Exhibition Society 8, 15, 17, *17*, 68, 207
Arts & Crafts movement 8, 21, 28
Arts & Crafts style 9
Ashbee, C.R. 8, 9
Auchenibert, Killearn 160, 162
—dining room *163*
—morning room *164*
—staircase *164*
Baillie Scott, M.H. 7, 18, 37, 72, 218
baldacchino 101, 103, 104
Ball, A.S., Berlin 150
—dining room for *150*, 152
banners *90*
barometer *200*
Bassett-Lowke, W.J. 133, 155, 195, 196, 198, *200*, 203, 204, 206, 208, *211*, 212, 215, *215*, *216*, *217*
Bassett-Lowke, Mrs. W.J. 204
Bassett-Lowke family *192*
Bauer, Leopold *72*
Bauhaus 218
Beardsley, Aubrey 9
bed 19, *38*, 39, 75, *84*, *116*, *138*, *142*
bedroom suite 14
Beethoven Frieze 68
Behrens, Peter 216, *217*
bench *12*, *22*, *82*
Bertsch, Karl 33, 34
billiards table *60*, *136*
billiards marker-board *65*, *136*
Blackie, Walter W. 74, 115, 121, 122, 125, 130
bookcase *12*, 14, *15*, 21, *22*, 51, 53, 56, *58*, *80*, *83*, *99*
Breuer, Marcel 198
Brown, George Washington 23
Brückmann, H., dining room for 33, *34*, 37
Buchanan Street Tea Rooms, Glasgow 23, 25, 27, 30
—dining room *23*
—Ladies' Tea Room *23*, 25
—Luncheon Room 25
—Smokers' Gallery 25
Burnet, John 154
Burrough & Watt *60*
cabinet 14, *21*, 32, 34, *34*, 68, 69, *70*, 75, *86*, *87*, 88, *129*, 130, *140*, *144*, *146*, *178*, *196*, *215*, *216*
Candida Cottage, Roade, near Northampton 208, 209, 211, *211*
candlestick *129*, *141*, *154*, *200*
carpet 104, 135, 136
cash desk *106*
Cave, Mr, 204
chair *13*, 27, 28, *29*, *31*, *32*, *43*, *47*, 52, 53, *55*, *64*, 69, *82*, *84*, 88, *88*, *91*, *93*, *96*, 98, 102, 104, *106*, *107*, *109*, *116*, *118*, 124, *126*, *127*, 129, *131*, *133*, *136*, 137, *140*, *141*, *143*, 144, *144*, 148, *150*, *154*, 160, *162*, 167, *167*, *168*, 175, *177*, 179, *180*, *183*, *184*, *186*, *197*, *201*, *207*, *208*, *209*, *215*
chandelier *105*

chest of drawers 20, *139*
cheval mirror 55, *55*, 56, *59*, *84*, *119*, *213*
chimneypiece *10*, *11*
choir stalls *49*
clock 110, *127*, *133*, *150*, *178*, *179*, *199*, *215*
Cochrane, Major 135
couch 116, *127*, 129, *138*
Craig, John 162
Craigie Hall, Glasgow *11*, 12
—library 12, *12*
—Music Room *34*, 36
Cranston, Catherine 23, 25, 27, 61, 101, 135, 144, 160, 165, 179, 184, 206
cupboard *15*, *116*, *202*
curtains 137
Cutting, Mrs 204
Daly's Department Store 112
Darmstadt 70
d'Aronco 89
Davidson, William 13, 14, 17, 21, *21*, 23, 32, 158, *216*
Davidson Jr, William 79
Day, L.F. 9
decorated frieze 34
Dekorative Kunst 33, 37, 69, 112, 122
Derngate, 78, Northampton 195, 196, *196*, *197*, 198, *200*, 202, 203, 206, 208, *214*, 215, *215*,
—bathroom 204
—dining room *193*, 211
—garden elevation *194*
—guest bedroom *194*, *201*, *202*, 204, 212, *212*, *213*
—hall *192*, 204, *216*, *217*
—main bedroom *193*, 204
—staircase *194*, *199*, 204
Design & Industries Association 195
desk 21, *22*, 53, *54*, *70*, *80*, 88, *90*, 94, *129*, 130, *142*, *174*
De Stijl 133
Deutsche Kunst und Dekoration 69
Deutscher Werkbund 195
Diack, Michael *70*, *99*
display cabinet *63*, *90*
door *110*, *164*
door canopy *187*
doorway *169*
Douglas, William *178*, *179*, *189*
dovecote *113*
draughtman's desk *179*
Dresdener Werkstätten für Handwerkskunst *124*, 125, 152
dresser 135, *148*, *177*
Drive, The, Northampton 211
—dining room *212*
Dunglass Castle, Bowling 56, 58, *59*
easel *177*
Ednie, John 191
fender *85*
fireplace *11*, *12*, *36*, *47*, 52, 53, *54*, *64*, *67*, *73*, *74*, 75, *78*, *81*, *83*, *86*, *96*, *107*, *108*, *110*, *111*, 112, *113*, *114*, *122*, *123*, 137, *144*, *147*, 157, 158, *163*, *179*, *194*, 206
fireplace ingle *136*, 161
fireplace cabinet *122*
fitted furniture *81*
—alcove seat 121
—cupboards *34*, 119
—glazed cabinet *96*
—seating *60*, *111*, *146*

—settle *86*
—wardrobes *118*
Florentine Terrace, 6. *See* Southpark Avenue
flower stand *67*
Four Queens, The 181
Franklin, W. *200*, *201*, *211*
garden seat *189*, *113*
Gauld, David *13*, 14
Gillespie, J. Gaff 191
Gimson, Ernest 9, 209
Gladsmuir, Kilmacolm 14, *15*, 21, 22, 79
—nursery *19*, 25
Glasgow Art Club 11, *11*
Glasgow Herald building, Mitchell Street 12, 14, *20*, *21*
Glasgow International Exhibition (1901) 76
—Exhibition stand for Francis Smith *77*
—Exhibition stand for the Glasgow School of Art 76, *77*
—Exhibition stand for Messrs. Rae Brothers *77*
—Exhibition stand for Pettigrew & Stephens *76*
Glasgow Exhibition (1911) 183
Glasgow School of Art 7, 20, 32, 40, *44*, *47*, *130*, *131*, *170*, *178*
—Architectural School *170*
—Boardroom 43, *44*, 152, *153*, *154*
—Composition room *173*
—East corridor *44*
—Entrance Hall *44*
—Headmaster's (now Director's) Room 40, 43, *44*, 48
—Ladies' Common Room *177*
—Lecture Theatre *170*, 171
—Library *16*, 144, 150, 153, 165, *170*, 172, 173, *173*, 174, *174*, 174, 175, *176*, *177*, 179, 184, 190
—Life modelling Room *170*
—loggia *173*
—Masters' Room *174*
—Museum *44*, 171
—refectory *173*
—West staircase *172*
Glasgow, University of 154
—Hunterian Art Gallery 158, 159
Glebe Place, Chelsea 195
Gourock Parish Church, Strathclyde *49*, *149*
grate 137
Grenander, Alfred 150, 151
Gropius, Walter 218
Guild and School of Handicraft 8
Guthrie & Wells 14, 15, *15*, *17*, *20*, 21, 25
hat, coat and shoe rack *126*
hat, coat and umbrella stand *30*, *63*, 133
hat hooks *134*
Haus eines Kunstfreundes 85, 115, 121, 146
—bedroom 74
—competition *29*
—drawing room *74*
—elevation of a bedroom wall *73*
—elevation of the south wall of the hall *71*
—main staircase 74
—music room 74, *74*, 88
—perspective of the dining room *71*
—reception room 74
—schoolroom 74, *74*
—windows *73*
Heart of the Rose 90
Henderson, A. Graham 164, 181
Henneberg, Hugo 69, *99*
Henderson, John 18, 21
Hevesi, Ludwig 96
Hill House, The, Helensburgh 7, 8, *38*, 75, *114*, 115, 116, 117, *118*, *119*, 121, *121*, 122, *122*, 123, *123*, 124, 125 *126*, *127*, *129*, *133*, 137, 169, *169*, *189*
—billiards room 115
—cloakroom 115
—day nursery 121
—dining room *118*, 122, 137
—drawing room 115, 117, *133*
—hall *116*
—library 115, *116*
—lighting 117
—main bedroom *114*, *116*, *118*, 121, 124
—playroom 121
Hislop, David 162
Hoffmann, Joseph 8, 68, 69, 94, *99*, 191, 218
Holy Trinity Church, Bridge of Allan, near Stirling 149, *149*, *150*
Honeyman, John 12
Honeyman & Keppie 11, 30
Honeyman, Keppie & Mackintosh 191
Hope, Henry 162
Horstmann, Sidney *200*
—bedroom for 206
Hous'hill, Nitshill, Glasgow 125, 133, *134*, 135, 146, *147*, *148*, 179
—billiards room *134*, 136, *136*
—blue bedroom 137, *139*, *140*, *141*
—card room *180*
—dining room *134*, *146*
—drawing room 125, 144, *144*, *146*, 147
—flower stand *134*
—music room 125, 181
—vestibule *134*
—white bedroom (guest bedroom) 137, *139*, *141*, *142*, *143*
Howarth, Thomas 9, 12, 152, 160, 184, 202, 204
Hunterian Art Gallery, Glasgow. *See* Glasgow, University of, Art Gallery
inglenook *121*
Ingram Street Tea Rooms 56, *60*, 61, *62*, *63*, 165, 181, *184*
—balcony of the White Dining Room *60*
—Billiards Room *60*, *166*
—Chinese Room 184, *185*, 186, 187, 203
—Cloister Room 57, 61, *62*, 184, 187, 188, *188*, 189
—Ladies' Dressing Room *65*
—Ladies' Rest Room 181, *182*, 183
—Oak room 152, 165, *166*, 167, *167*, *168*, 183
—Oval room 147, 164, 181, *182*, *183*, 184
—White Dining Room 56, *61*, *64*
International Exhibition of Modern Decorative Art, Turin (1902) 25, 89, *93*
—Glasgow School of Art exhibit 89
—Rose boudoir 88, 89, *90*, *91*, 92
—Scottish Exhibition Area *90*
Japanese Style 9
jewel box *17*, 21
Jones, F. 209, *212*
Kensington Restaurant, Glasgow 112
Keppie, Jessie *17*, 21
Keppie, John 11, 12, 19, *20*, 154, 164
Kilmacolm. *See* Gladsmuir; Windyhill
Kingsborough Gardens, 14, Glasgow 85, 88
—dining room fireplace 85
—drawing room 85, *86*
kitchen dresser *161*
Klimt, Gustav 68, 69
Koch, Alexander 70
Kornwolf, J.D. 9
Lady Artists' Club, Blythswood Square, Glasgow 169, *169*
lamp 133, *133*, 194
lantern 136
Le Corbusier 198
light fittings 137
lighting 156, 158, 161
linen cabinet 21
linen cupboard 121
linen press *17*, 21, *21*
Little Hills, The 207
Logan, George 191

luggage stool *214*
Macdonald, Charles 56
Macdonald, Margaret 8, 17, *17*, 21, 32, 34, *34*, 49, *67*, 68, 69, *74*, 75, *76*, 88, 89, 92, 94, *96*, *99*, *105*, *122*, 123, *141*, 181, 207, 218
Maclehose, J. 37
MacNair, Frances 89
MacNair, Herbert 12, 89
Maeterlinck, Maurice 9, 92, 95
magazine stand *177*
Mains Street, 120, Glasgow 32, 49, *51*, *52*, 53, *53*, *54*, *55*, *56*, *57*, 158
—bedroom *51*, 54
—dining room *51*, 53
—drawing room 37, 49, *51*
—studio *51*, 54
mantelpiece *194*
Marmorek, Oskar 72
Martin, Alexander 8
Mason, Thomas 12
May Queen, The 57, *68*
McLaren Young, Andrew 158, 159, 160
meat safe *161*
mirror 65, *143*, *217*
Morris, William 9
Moscow Exhibition (1903) 88, *98*
Moser, Koloman 69, 191
Moss, The, Dumgoyne, near Killearn, Stirlingshire 121
—extension 168
Newbery, Fra 43, 89
Newbery, Jessie 85
newspaper rack *176*
New Ways, Northampton 215, 216
—study *217*
Olbrich, J.M. 70, 151
Opera of the Sea, The 97
Opera of the Wind, The 97
organ case *34*, *36*
organ screen 149, *149*, 150, *150*
organ stool *36*
'O ye, all ye that walk in Willowwood' 108
panel 34, *39*, *74*, 75, *76*, *90*, 94, *105*, *122*, 177
panelling 40, *40*, 69, 162
Part Seen, Imagined Part 25
periodical desk *174*, 175
Pettigrew & Stephens 76
Pevsner, Nikolaus 206, 218
piano *73*, 75, 76, 95, *95*
Pollokshields 12
Prutscher, Otto 191, 194, *215*
pulpit 43, 49, 149, *149*
Queen's Cross Church, Glasgow 23, 40, *41*, 43, 149, 175
Queen Margaret Medical College, Glasgow 19
—Museum *16*, 172
Rae Brothers 76
Regent Park Square, Glasgow 18, *18*, *19*
reredos *43*
Rietveld, Gerrit 133
roof timbers *40*
roof trusses *41*
Rossetti, Dante Gabriel 108
Rowat, Mrs 85
Russell, R.D. 209
St Vincent Street, 233, Glasgow *40*
Salmon Jr, James 191
Scotland Street School 7, 8
Scott, Gilbert 154
screen *101*, 144, *144*, 147, 149, 161, 167
service trolley *211*
settee *30*
settle *17*, 21, 32, *47*, *57*, 68, *88*, 199, *207*
Seven Princesses 92, 95
Shand, F.J. 162
sideboard *19*, *21*, *67*, *73*, *150*, *168*, *211*

Smith, Francis 8, 76
smoker's cabinet 32, 69, *99*, *196*
Southpark Avenue, 78, Glasgow 149, 154, 155, 158, 159, 160, *161*, 212, *216*
—bedroom 158
—demolition of 158
—drawing room 155, 156, 157
—hall 155
—reconstruction of 158, 159
—studio 156, 158
Spook School 12, *12*, 18, *23*
staircase screen *192*
stand for collection dish *43*
stool *107*, *127*, *167*, *214*
Studio, The 10, 18, 25, *28*, 33, 204
Sturrock, Mary Newbery 191, 195, 207
table *13*, *17*, *20*, *22*, 27, *28*, *29*, *30*, *31*, *32*, 34, *39*, *43*, 48, *52*, *54*, *56*, *60*, *63*, *80*, 82, *84*, *86*, *96*, *96*, *97*, *99*, *103*, 104, *106*, *108*, 111, *111*, *119*, *127*, 129, *129*, *130*, 136, *136*, *141*, *142*, *147*, *148*, 149, *149*, *150*, *153*, 158, *169*, 175, *176*, *177*, *178*, 179, *179*, *181*, *187*, *189*, *196*, *200*, *202*, *207*, *208*, *211*, *213*, *216*
Taylor, E.A. 191
telephone box 169
Toorop, Jan 9
towel rail *126*, *202*
umbrella stand *57*, *62*, *65*, *101*, *126*, *134*
Urban, Joseph 204
Utility designs 209
van der Rohe, Mies 198, 218
Vienna 191
Vienna Secession, Eighth Exhibition of (1900) 34, 37, *67*, 68, *68*
Voices of the Woods 207, *209*
Voysey, C.F.A. 8, 9, 218
Walberswick, Suffolk 191, 195, 207
wall-hangings 102
wall-mounted candelabra *209*
Walton, George 25, 27, 28, 37, *146*, 160
wardrobe *13*, *15*, *38*, 39, *55*, *56*, *75*, *200*, *201*, 215
Wärndorfer, Fritz 69, 89, *90*, *93*, 94
Wärndorfer Music Salon 9, 88, 94, 95
washstand *13*, *17*, *57*, *75*, *83*, *119*, *142*, *202*, *214*
Wassail, The, 57, *61*, *67*
Westdel, 2 Queen's Place, Glasgow *22*, 37, *38*
White, Gleeson 25, 33
White Cockade Tea Room 183
White Rose and the Red Rose, The 90
Whitfield, William 158, 159
Wiener Werkstätte 8
Wilkson, Heywood & Clark 203
Willow Tea Rooms, Sauchiehall Street, Glasgow 8, 101, *106*, *107*, *108*, *109*, 112, 125, *131*, *133*
—Back Saloon *101*, *102*, 103, 104
—Billiards Room *104*, 111, *111*
—The Dug-Out 101, 112, 206, 207, 0207, 208, *208*, *209*
—Front Saloon *100*, *101*, 102, 103, 104, 147
—Gallery *102*, 103
—Gallery Tea Rooms 105
—restoration of 113
—Room de Luxe or Ladies' Room *103*, *105*, 108, 109, *110*, 111, 218
—Smoking Room *106*, 111
Windyhill, Kilmacolm 7, 8, *22*, 23, 76, 79, *80*, *81*, 88, *113*, 137
—bedroom 76, *81*
—dining room *80*
—drawing room 79, *808*, *81*
—hall *78*, 79
—lighting 82
—staircase *78*, 79, *81*
Wright, Frank Lloyd 10
Zeitschrift für Innendekoration 70
Zeroch, Paul 72